He, Me,

❧ and ❧

My Donkeys

HERBERT MAYS

as told to

RICHARD SALCIDO

ISBN 978-1-64300-382-5 (Paperback)
ISBN 978-1-64300-383-2 (Digital)

Copyright © 2018 HERBERT MAYS
All rights reserved
First Edition

Covenant Books, Inc.
11661 Hwy 707
Murrells Inlet, SC 29576
www.covenantbooks.com

I dedicate this book to my precious wife, Becky, the love of my life; to my son, Lee, and my daughter, Lesley, both my pride and joy; and to my grandchildren Brittany, Brayleigh, and Cainan, the apples of my eye. I further dedicate this book to the memory of two pastors who sowed significantly into my life, Reverend Paul Baggett and Reverend Bill Cowan, along with his wife, Effie.

FOREWORD

Knowing Pastor Herbert Mays for over twenty years, I consider it a profound honor to write this foreword for his autobiography. As an evangelist, I have preached in a multitude of churches throughout the country for the past eighteen years, where I encountered many different congregations and pastors. I can honestly say that few match Pastor Mays in genuine love and devotion to God and people. Pastor Mays does not adhere to schedules or timetables during church services, nor does he confine the Holy Spirit to an obscure prayer room somewhere in the church building. God is completely free to move as He wills to lovingly touch people in need.

He, Me, and My Donkeys is a book that reveals the courage, character, and commitment that Pastor Mays possesses. His courage on the battlefield warrants recognition. His commitment to the men under his command will inspire all who read about it, because he left no man behind. Pastor Mays displays this same God-given commitment for the people who attend his church. With character above reproach, he is one of the most upright men I know. I am blessed to say that Pastor Mays is my dear friend.

He, Me, and My Donkeys is a great read. When I first began to peruse its passages, I only intended to browse through a few pages because I had many things on my to-do list that day. However, I ended up reading this book from cover to cover in one sitting. Pastor Mays's life story is inspiring. The vignettes contained within are touching, encouraging and enlightening. I thoroughly enjoyed reading *He, Me, and My Donkeys*. It was time well spent.

Reverend Kenneth R. Cowan

PREFACE

This book is my autobiography which includes several stories of my life experiences, some humorous, some dismaying, some inspiring, and some miraculous. My life story conveys how God took me when I was seemingly insignificant and thought I had no ability and used me to benefit the life of others. I have written this book to give God glory for taking a homeless high school dropout with low expectations and using me to positively impact the life of people around the world.

The book reveals God's greatness that He could take someone from a low station in life and bestow on me an anointing to bless people. I share my story of what God has done for me. I hope every reader realizes that with God all things are possible. If we really submit ourselves to God, He can take ordinary people and do extraordinary things. God with His power can use us if we submit to Him and give Him the glory.

In addition, the book also offers a glimpse into rural America in the 1950s, the early years of the Vietnam War from a firsthand account, America's transformation in the 1960s, and a glance into foreign cultures.

My children asked me for years to write a book of my life so that they could have a historical account for their remembrance and to pass on to their children as a legacy. In addition to this, many friends urged me over the years to compile into a book all the stories from my life experiences that I tell during my sermons. I finally decided to do this to show how great God is and what He can do in a life submitted to Him.

I present this autobiography to the best of my recollection and apologize for any inaccuracies. My hope is that everyone who reads this book will glean from it the fact that God wants to use everyone to do something for His kingdom. We all have a different calling on our life as well as different abilities. I'm not a great orator or a flashy preacher. However, I yield to the Holy Spirit as did others who weren't that well educated or refined such as Smith Wigglesworth, now referred to as the Father of Faith.

God had His hand on my life even when I didn't serve Him. I believe this because my grandmother girded my life with hours and hours of her prayers. She also imparted to me Bible scripture and much confession that God would use me. Though it took many years, all this finally came to fruition in my life.

After doing this project, I gained a greater realization of how much God cared for me even when I wasn't interested in Him. I had a death sentence, so to speak, when in the Vietnam War. God spared me and wrought many accomplishments with my life. God had His hand on my life, protected me, and encouraged me. Even when I coached sports, I always felt that I could do it well and win, because something out there watched over me and empowered me.

Another insight gained was how powerful words can be in people's life. Agreement in faith and speaking positive words yielded power. During difficult times in my life, friends expressed doubt and discouragement to me. Thank God that my wife, Becky, encouraged me with words of faith, as we made it through every situation believing that we could succeed. Faith and positive confession produced powerful results.

I hope this book helps those who have tried unsuccessfully to resolve problems that they experienced. Reach out and submit to God. He has everyday people out there who can help you. Your resolution doesn't have to come from a minister. Mine didn't.

This literary work came about when I announced in church in 2017 that I would finally write a book which included my stories. I stated that my first step would be to find a writer to help me because I didn't have the necessary skills to write a book on my own. I had no idea how to procure a writer. Miraculously, after the church service, one of our attendees, Richard Salcido (Rick), told me that he wrote well and would help me with the book. I accepted his offer. Not knowing how or where to start, I genuinely felt that this would be an inept venture. Who would be interested in reading about my life anyway?

A few weeks later, Rick gave me a digital recorder and asked me to start by telling my Vietnam War story. Still pessimistic about the whole endeavor, I procrastinated for weeks expecting this effort to fizzle out and fade into obscurity. Fortunately, Rick politely pressed me every Wednesday and Sunday after church service about the recording. Consequently, I decided that I should at least give it a try. Feeling awkward about sitting in a room by myself and talking into a recorder, I only managed to sputter out a nine-and-a-half-minute recording. This further confirmed my notion that this project would probably go nowhere.

Then something unexpected and noteworthy happened. Rick transcribed that short recording into paragraphs and generated several questions per paragraph. He then set an appointment to do an interview with me. As he asked the interview questions, I comfortably answered with in-depth responses as my life story began to flow out of me and into the recorder. This interview/conversation style was just what I needed to get my story out. Now we were cooking with gas! I started to feel good about the project.

I travailed for weeks about what to call the book. During the middle of one night, I woke up with the title *He, Me, and My Donkeys* running through my mind. Because the book involved God, His hand on my life, and how my donkeys help me deal with PTSD and stress, I chose this name for the book.

As we progressed, people read what we had completed so far. To my surprise, people found the book intriguing, humorous, and touching. At this point, my outlook on the project became very positive. I now believed that anybody who read the book could be encouraged. No matter where they were in life or what their education level, they could bless humanity. If people used what I call the FROG (Fully Rely on God) approach in life, then God would use them.

ACKNOWLEDGMENTS

To begin, I wish to thank God for His hand upon my life and for bringing the right people across my path to encourage me and help me to accomplish this book. God saw ability in me that I didn't. He is the only Father that I have ever had. He is my spiritual Father as well as my earthly Father in my opinion. He showed me love when my earthly father didn't. Without God, I would absolutely be nothing. I give Him all the glory.

Next, words cannot express my love for and gratitude to my wife, Becky. She stood by me despite all my faults and failures in life. She always believed that we would somehow make it through every tough time together as a team. She never doubted anything, saying if God said it, then we were going to do it. Second to God only, Becky is my bedrock who covers me in prayer and encouragement continually.

I wish to thank my son, Lee, and daughter, Lesley, for being a ray of joy in my life and encouraging me to write this book. May God always smile on their life.

I express my deepest love and appreciation to my grandmother Ma Lincoln. I look forward to the day when I see her again. The impact that her words, prayers, and faith had on my life cannot be measured. Her genuine love and kindness toward me inspire me to reach out and help others.

I thank all my friends over the years who encouraged me to put all my life stories into a book. I especially thank Cathy Coyne for her gentle yet persistent persuasion for me to do this. Her confidence in me encouraged me to attempt this project.

I also give my thanks to Gary Hartt and Bill Sealy, my army buddies from the Vietnam War. They helped recall and clarify events that took place fifty years ago that I suppressed for decades.

I give a special thanks to Rick Salcido who has been a joy, a blessing, a ray of hope, and an encouragement. Without him, this endeavor wouldn't have been possible. Using his wonderful way with words, he put my life story to pen and paper in a way that made readers smile, laugh, frown, and weep. I appreciate all the hours he put in for the sake of this book. I am grateful for his dedication, hard work, and numerous days spent with me on this project. I don't have words to thank him enough and to express how much his interest and efforts meant to me.

Finally, I thank Reverend Paul Baggett and Reverend Bill Cowan for the impartations that they put into my life spiritually.

CHAPTER 1

Ambush!

In late January 1967, the ninety-degree Vietnam heat strangled us, as two soldiers and I patrolled for about three days on a long-range reconnaissance patrol (LRRP). We ran low on food. If ninety degrees didn't sound bad, it combined with 80 percent humidity and a triple canopy jungle to create an oven-baked environment that felt more like one hundred twenty degrees. We hacked our way through the thick vegetation using a machete as sweat drenched our bodies and weapons and equipment weighed us down. We constantly drank water to stay alive. Even when we reached a clearing, we found no mercy. We still hacked our way through razor-sharp seven-foot-tall elephant grass. Everything here cut, poked, or bit us whether plant, insect, or animal.

The morning of the third day, January 29, we entered Hamlet 6 Chanh and bought food from the villagers. We had to use extreme caution to find out if they were friendly or not. We spent time with the South Vietnamese villagers and knew how to deal with them. Constantly putting items from our C rations into grass sacks, we took the food to local villages to help the people. We gladly did it.

The air seemed hotter than usual that day as we left the little village. Anxious to get back to base camp, we came out of the jungle into a big open area that had a decent road running through it. This road ran north to south and went past a South Vietnamese hospital located on the outskirts of Hamlet 6 Chanh. Little did I know at the time, but this spot would change my life forever.

I had never physically seen the hospital before even though our map showed it. I wanted to check it out. As we made our way across the clearing, our radio operator spotted a large enemy unit off in the distance coming down the road. By their uniforms, I could tell that they were North Vietnamese Army regular troops, not the guerilla fighting Vietcong. Perhaps they brought their wounded to this hospital for treatment. I didn't think we could safely make a run for it back into the jungle because we went too far out into the open area. Fortunately, they hadn't seen us. We turned off the radio and hid in a gully about fifty feet from the road. The enemy passed by unaware of our presence. With the enemy no longer in sight, we left the area.

Extremely hungry and only about two kilometers (klicks) from base camp, we cautiously headed home. I looked forward to an evening off, a decent meal, and some sleep. We arrived at the Dau Tieng Base Camp about two o'clock in the afternoon. When we got back to our company area, I reported what we saw to Captain Ken Both. I think the captain suspected that the North Vietnamese Army would retrieve their wounded from the hospital later that night. He ordered me to take my sixteen-man squad out that evening and set up an ambush on the road leading to the hospital. Dirty, I wanted to clean up. Hungry, I wanted a good meal. Tired, I wanted a beer and some sleep that night. Out for three days, I just got in, and the captain sent me right back out to do an ambush. I left, irritated and upset, to prepare for the first and only ambush that I would oversee.

Planning the ambush during the afternoon of January 29, 1967.

In hindsight, Captain Both made a wise decision to send me back out there to lead the ambush patrol. I knew the area and saw the enemy. As a result, I had a strong suspicion that we would encounter them again that night. I made sure my squad recognized that fact too. Despite my youth, the captain had a lot of respect for and confidence in me. He trusted me to do the mission right. I loved the army, took my duty and training seriously, and had good instincts having lived on my own for two years as a teenager before joining the army. A different squad might have gone out not expecting to engage the enemy. Who knows what would have happened to them.

I had everybody clean their weapons. Stateside we trained with the M14 rifle. Here in Vietnam, we got the new M16 rifle but received no training on it. One thing we did know, the M16 jammed, a lot! We doubled up on our ammo. I coordinated our mission support. I got with the artillery and told them where we would set up the ambush that night. I had gone into the jungle many nights before and lost my bearing, ending up in a different spot than where I thought. But that day, I took out my map and pinpointed where we would emplace, since I had been there earlier in the day and the hospital provided an accurate reference point. Finally, I told the men that I strongly felt that we would have some action that night. I just knew, so everyone needed to be physically and mentally ready.

We left base camp between five and six o'clock that evening. As dusk dropped its dark cloak over the landscape, we set up the ambush about twenty yards west of the road with our backs to the jungle, which sat silently several yards behind us. Our ambush line stretched about fifty feet from one end to the other. David Burkholz, my best friend, manned the M60 machine gun at the north end of the ambush line. Bill Sealy with his M60 protected our south flank. I took a position in the middle, with the medic, forward observer, and the radio operator nearby.

I spent many uneventful nights in the jungle where I didn't sense that anything would happen. This night felt different. This night had an eerie feel to it. I sensed that we would encounter the enemy in a tough way. Normally, in the jungle you would hear a little noise at night. However, nothing moved as if to warn us. The ghostly silence brooded and grieved over us.

The deathly still, dark, hot, and uncanny air begged for our attention as if it wanted to say, "Watch out!"

The men sensed it too. At this point, we all knew that fate had something difficult in store for us this night. About thirty minutes after setting up the ambush, we heard the enemy coming down the road three hundred yards away. When I looked through the night vision scope, I saw Vietcong about a hundred yards off.

As their three lead soldiers passed by, I started the ambush by yelling, "I'm blowing you to h—— tonight!" I shot all three dead with my M16.

The fight started about eight o'clock. I thought, at first, that the enemy was squad size, but they turned out to be larger than we were. To make matters worse, most of the enemy veered off the road and walked up on our left flank where David manned the M60 machine gun. After I shot the first three Vietcong soldiers, the enemy shot David repeatedly in his torso area.

Outnumbered, I formed the squad from an ambush line into a defensive circle about thirty feet across as the enemy moved around behind us. At first the excitement and adrenaline rush of it all exhilarated me. Reality quickly set in as I realized this was for keeps. During combat, you think only about survival. The soldiers who concentrated and focused survived. The guy thinking about Aunt Susie or about his girlfriend back home usually returned in a body bag. As a sergeant, my priority was to keep the men alive. I likened it to a football coach although this was by no means a game. My job was to put them in a position to win. I believed that if I took care of my soldiers, then I would make it too.

During the chaos, Tyrus O'Ruke got separated from the group and fought from a solitary position. After a while, his M16 jammed. Out of grenades and unable to defend himself, he hid under a dead Vietcong body, waiting for rescue. We fought off the attackers for an hour or so, firing everything we had hot and heavy at first. At times, one of them would break through our line. We shot or killed him by hand-to-hand combat. Later, we started conserving our ammo shooting at deliberate targets.

It seemed that the enemy got reinforced. I didn't know if that was true, but it felt like it because they just kept on coming at us. (I found out later that an estimated force of eighty Vietcong had fought us there that night.) By this time, I had destroyed the night vision scope with my .45-caliber pistol to keep it out of enemy hands. Also, our M16s began to jam. Our situation didn't look good. Thank God that our M60 machine guns kept firing.

I radioed Captain Both and exclaimed, "We're surrounded by the enemy! I don't think we can hold out on our own! We desperately need some help!"

The captain replied, "Roger. We'll get to you as soon as we can but first we have to get permission from the base command to send a rescue force. It might take a while. You will have to hold on as best you can until then."

That was not what I wanted to hear. Highly upset, I replied with vigorous, colorful language. Captain Both then told me to call in artillery.

The rescue force assembled about nine thirty. Base command hesitated to give them the okay to leave for fear that the Vietcong was using my squad as bait to ambush the larger rescue force as it came to our aid. At the base camp perimeter, Gary Hartt waited with the rest of the rescue force. From the berm, he could see the muzzle flashes and tracers of the fire fight about two klicks off in the distance. He only saw green Vietcong tracers. He didn't see red US tracers because our M16s had jammed. Base command finally gave them the go-ahead about eleven thirty.

I always tried to tell my men the truth. About two hours into the fight, I told them relief would take a while and that we were calling in artillery close to our position. George O'Connor, our forward observer, brought the artillery to within fifty meters of our location. We called this danger close. To do this, he had to constantly communicate with the artillery by radio. The squawk of the radio gave away the specific location of his comrades. Therefore, he took up an isolated position away from ours so as not to further endanger the squad. From his vulnerable spot, George called in artillery protecting our position without regard for his own safety. In so doing, he saved our lives and earned the Silver Star for gallantry in combat.

When the artillery rounds came in, they hit exactly where we needed them to. The rounds dropped one at a time encircling our position. The men and I felt better about the situation. I began to believe that we would make it out alive. As the blasts illuminated the area, we could see the enemy trying to maneuver toward us at various spots. Again, the enemy would get into our perimeter here and there and someone would shoot or kill them in hand-to-hand combat.

During the fighting, we had a man get captured. The Vietcong dragged him to a tree line some distance away and tortured him. We could hear him screaming as two Vietcong had him pinned up against a tree. I told the medic that I was going to get him back. The medic pleaded with me not to go. I promised these men that I would do everything in my power to get them all home and I meant it. I took some men, and we went out to rescue our comrade. We had to run through the artillery to get to him. The soldiers that came with me got the jump on the Vietcong and killed them with bayonets. I slung our wounded soldier over my shoulder, and we helped him run back to our position.

As we worked our way back through the artillery, an enemy grenade landed at my feet. The grenade exploded, spitting shrapnel in all directions and knocking me down. I didn't feel anything hit me. I quickly rose to my feet, picked up the wounded soldier, and continued running. Three other men got injured from the grenade too. In the confusion of explosions and chaos, we couldn't make it back to our defensive perimeter, so we made a new one.

I felt blood running down my leg. I reached around to feel the right side of my back and discovered that my uniform shirt was all tattered. Then I realized that the grenade had blown out that part of my body. I felt a gaping hole. I then knew that I was severely wounded. Even at that moment, I don't remember feeling pain or thinking that I would die.

About midnight, Captain Both along with a platoon from our company had gotten to us in five armored personnel carriers (APCs). As the rescue column approached, the Vietcong fired at them from the hospital in the hamlet. Gary who manned a .50-caliber machine gun on one of the APCs fired in return.

A lieutenant screamed at him, "That's a hospital in a friendly village. Do it again, I'll have you court martialed!"

Gary yelled back, "I don't think green tracers fired at me are very friendly, Lieutenant!"

With the enemy on the run and my squad scattered, our rescuers collected us up. Later, I had heard that at one spot they built a makeshift bridge to get across the large ditch that the artillery made around our position.

Pinned down for over four hours, my squad and I laid on the ground exhausted and wounded. (Bill got hit in the backside with shrapnel, which is still there today fifty years later. He spent a few weeks in a hospital and then got back in the war.) I couldn't move.

Jack Conrad, the soldier who drove our squad APC, came up to me and said, "Sarg, I got something for you. I brought you a six-pack of beer." He opened a can, and I took a drink. That was the last moment I remember of the ambush.

The company took us by APC to the Dau Tieng base camp aid station for triage. Don Smith, our company clerk, held a flashlight for the doctor who examined and treated us.

After looking at me, the doctor told a medic, "This boy will die in thirty minutes. Put him on a helicopter and send him to the morgue at Cu Chi."

It was about a forty-minute flight from Dau Tieng to the Cu Chi Base Camp by helicopter.

When I heard the doctor say that, I proclaimed, "If there is a God in Heaven, I will not die in Vietnam!" That was the last thing I remember of that night.

At the time, I didn't know much about the Bible, but Proverbs 18:21 said, "Death and life are in the power of the tongue. And those who love it will eat its fruit." A person who indulged in death talk reaped death. A person who indulged in life talk reaped life.

As an overpowering shadow devoured me, all sights, sounds, light, and color faded to an ominous black. I slid into a deep pit of dense darkness devoid of consciousness. None of my senses worked. Barely aware of my existence, I floated in an unending expanse of nothingness. The time spent in this dark chasm yielded no memories, a complete gap in my life.

CHAPTER 2

Beginnings

Surrounded by darkness, my thoughts emerged as the only consciousness that seemed to exist. But even my thoughts appeared primitive and superficial, nothing profound or deep. I had no idea of my situation. I felt suspended in a warm pool of water. I floated motionless, drifting about. I heard what seemed like a drum. *Thump, thump. Thump, thump.* From time to time, I heard muffled sounds. Suddenly, great turmoil devoured me, as did confusion and fright. A bright light violently confronted me. My eyelids flinched and convulsed as my eyes painfully adjusted to this new sensation. Simultaneously, I felt a sharp smack to my backside as I cried out for the first time. On September 18, 1946, my mother gave birth to me, Herbert Lee Mays, in an old farmhouse that sat unimpressively fifteen miles southwest of Nashville, Tennessee in the farming community of Bellevue. I was the fourth-born child out of five that my parents had.

My daddy stood about 6 feet tall and weighed 250 pounds, an imposing figure to a little boy. Daddy and I never had a close relationship. In my eyes, he went about an arrogant, self-centered, and unloving man. He and my two oldest brothers formed a clique. What time he had for his children, he spent with the two oldest boys and with Joann, his firstborn. I never felt loved, appreciated, or even wanted by Daddy. To my recollection, he never offered me any expression of love nor kind gesture, nothing. A very hard man, he provided for some of us only out of obligation rather than love.

A vivid memory of Daddy, one day as a small boy I dumped some potatoes from a fifty-pound bag that we always had in the kitchen. I played with them like little cars and trucks upon the kitchen floor. I had them all spread out as my own little metropolis.

Daddy came through the house and said, "Herbie, pick those potatoes up and put them back into the sack and leave them alone." He then went outside.

I continued to play with the potatoes. About thirty minutes later, Daddy came back into the house and saw me still playing with them.

He scolded, "I told you to put those potatoes up!"

Well, I still didn't do it. When Daddy came back through the kitchen again a short while later, I still played with the potatoes sprawled out on the floor. Daddy went out to the wood pile and got a three-foot-long piece of kindling. Reentering the house, he beat me on the back with that switch until blood soaked my shirt, as I screamed and thrashed about.

Reacting to the commotion, Mom pleaded desperately, "Stop now! Stop, you're going to kill him!"

I concluded in my heart that if Daddy ever beat me like that again, I would kill him. We kept a shotgun in the house. If he ever did that to me a second time, I would make sure it was the last. Fortunately, Daddy never beat me like that again. For my part, I never gave him any reason to. Unpleasant memories of Daddy were typical for me. I neither had an enjoyable moment with him nor got an encouraging word or compliment from him.

On the other hand, I remembered my mom, Estelle, as a kind, hardworking woman. A great cook and selfless woman, she would bake a pie and cut it into six pieces instead of seven.

She would then say, "I don't like that kind of pie. The rest of you eat it."

She in truth made sure each of us received a bigger slice. Mom, a full-blooded Cherokee woman, had dark skin, hair, and eyes. She stood average height and build for a woman of that time. My younger sister and I had a closer relationship with Mom than we had with Daddy.

Mom worked on the side to make a little money for the family. A good seamstress, she made most of the clothes for our family, dresses for the girls and shirts for the guys. When I was about eight years old, she started cleaning house for Mr. and Mrs. Herndon. Mr. Herndon was an executive of the Baird Ward Printing Company in Nashville. They lived in a beautiful house not too far from our farm. Everyone seemed to love my mom because of her bubbly personality. Mom never met a stranger and made friends easily.

Joann, the oldest, hailed nine years before me. The second mama of the family, she lived life as one of the sweetest young ladies on the face of the earth. Smart, as well as nurturing and caring, she left for nursing school after graduating from high school. Nine years old at the time, I cried because I didn't want her to go. She served as a second lieutenant in the army medical corps for two years after becoming a nurse. During that time, she met her husband, an army pilot. They got out of the military and moved to North Carolina in 1959. I loved my oldest sister, Joann, very much.

Born second, my oldest brother acted arrogant and self-centered like Daddy. Seven and a half years older than me, he had the attitude that everything was all about him. He never paid me much attention when I was a child. A smart student and a good athlete, he played quarterback for the high school and got a scholarship to the University of Tennessee Martin. After college, he went back to farming. My oldest brother completely disowned me when I was fourteen. Years later, I visited him at his farm in Middle Tennessee. When I walked up and said hello, he never even looked up to acknowledge me as he worked on a hay rake. I had no idea why he treated me like that most of my life.

Next came my second brother, Linton, the third-born child six years before me. The bad boy of the outfit, Linton always rebelled without a cause. Shorter than most his age, yet a scrappy fighter, he loved to argue and would fight someone in an instant. Linton mouthed off quickly, a self-centered person as well. A rough guy who drank a lot and drove hot rods, he was no stranger to the jails of

Davidson County. I remembered my parents getting him out of jail on different occasions.

Finally, my youngest sister was born a year after me. A beautiful girl with olive skin, dark black hair, and dark black eyes like coal, she and I formed a close bond as children, which unfortunately faded as we got older. She had a close bond with Mom though that lasted a lifetime. Later in life, Mom lived with her in Georgia. When Mom died, I went to Georgia for the funeral. My younger sister treated me cordially but more like a guest than a brother.

Because of the six-year gap between the older children and us two youngest, I felt like an outsider in my own family, as if Daddy and the older boys begrudged us for being born. For some strange reason, it seemed as if two different families shared the same house and kept to themselves for the most part.

My grandfather built the house that we lived in which Daddy inherited along with the farm before I was born. Over thirty years old and in poor condition without indoor plumbing, our house sat back in a hollow off Poplar Creek Road near Highway 100. A long dirt drive led from the paved road to the house. Seven of us squeezed into this one-thousand-square-foot house which had a kitchen, living room, large master bedroom, and smaller second bedroom. A solitary light bulb dangled at the end of electrical wire from each ceiling. A pull of the chain dimly illuminated the room. The house never had any paint on it, just old exposed wood. The tin roof pinged loudly in the rain.

My youngest sister and I shared a twin bed in the master bedroom where my parents slept. My two older brothers shared the second bedroom. My oldest sister had a makeshift bedroom in the attic. We used the wood stove to cook our meals and heat the house during the winter. During the summer, we kept the windows open to cool the house.

We got fresh water daily from a well outside. We put a long tube down into the well. Somehow water filled up the tube. After extracting the tube from the well, a pull of a lever released the water into a pail. I didn't know how the tube worked. I never gave it a second thought. I just took it for granted.

To bathe, we made several trips to the well to fill up the tub. Before pouring the water into the tub, though, we heated it on the wood stove. Because it was quite an endeavor, we only bathed once a week. During the week, we put water into a pail and washed from that. Sometimes I walked to Aunt Rosetta (my mom's sister) and Uncle Clifton's house to take a bath because they had indoor plumbing. During the summer when my younger sister and I were small, Joann put a tub in the yard and fill it with water. She then gave us a bath outside, a cool refreshing reprieve from the humid summer heat.

In the house, we drank water from a two-gallon bucket using a dipper. We all used the dipper but never washed it after each use. Again, something we took for granted, never giving it a second thought. Some winter mornings we woke to frozen drinking water because the temperature got that cold. We had to put the bucket on the wood-burning stove and build a fire to melt the frozen water to get a drink. The wood-burning stove somewhat heated the kitchen and the living room of the house in the winter. But the rest of the house remained cold. In the summer, the house was hot. We didn't have air conditioning, only screens on the windows which we kept open day and night.

Our farm was seventy-two acres of rolling hills with pasture and woods. Although a farmer, Daddy also worked as a carpenter. He and my uncle built houses when the opportunity arose. We had a flatbed truck used for farming and a plain family sedan. On our farm, we raised cattle and hogs and planted vegetables in a huge garden. We had a couple milk cows as well. We also worked on a neighboring farm planting and harvesting tobacco. We only grew a small amount of tobacco on our own farm.

Each day, we got up early and went to school. When we got home that afternoon, we worked the farm. I remember picking and hoeing the garden, feeding animals, and taking up hay. My main job was caring for the hogs, but we did whatever needed doing. None of us had a set list of chores to do daily. We farmed until I was about eleven years old. Then Daddy started selling off the animals and worked more outside the farm.

Mom canned everything in jars because we didn't have a refrigerator or freezer. We children peeled apples and prepared the food for Mom to can. From hogs, we got ham and bacon. Daddy and my older brothers salted and flavored the pork with various spices. Then they hung it in a smoke house to cure so the meat didn't spoil. Whenever we needed bacon or pork, someone went out to the smoke house and cut portions big enough for what we wanted that day.

Back then in Bellevue, most households didn't have telephones or televisions. We gathered in the evening and listened to the radio. On Friday and Saturday nights, we enjoyed the *Grand Ole Opry*. I especially looked forward to Saturday nights. Earlier in the day, Mom sent me to the store to get a loaf of sliced bread. For Saturday night dinner, we had bologna sandwiches on store-bought sliced bread with homemade chili. During the week, Mom made either biscuits or cornbread from scratch, so I considered sliced bread from the store a special treat. I always looked forward to Saturday nights. It was a big deal to me.

Every Sunday, we attended the only Baptist church in Bellevue at that time. The church had a congregation of about one hundred people. It didn't have children's church or youth groups back then. Everybody, regardless of age, sat in the main sanctuary for the regular service. During the summer, however, on Thursday nights, children went to the church and played basketball. Only about a dozen children ever came. On Sunday afternoons, Mom and her ten surviving brothers and sisters with their families gathered for dinner at somebody's house. (My grandmother had thirteen children. Two of which died before I was born.) Everybody pitched in. We ate good food. Grown-ups talked and visited. Children ran around and played. Families, neighbors, and communities were tight-knit during the 1940s and 1950s, unlike America today.

Every Thanksgiving, several farmers from the community brought their hogs to our farm and slaughtered them in preparation for the holiday meal. That way the ham was fresh since most people didn't have refrigerators. I didn't know why they concentrated on our farm. But each year, they came and helped each other slaughter the hogs. We ate pork for Thanksgiving rather than turkey.

As a little child, I thought everyone lived this way. We modestly had food, clothing, and shelter but wanted for nothing. Not having anything to compare my life to, I didn't think of my family as poor. I didn't remember any of us complaining about not having enough. At Christmas, we put up a Christmas tree. Each child got a sack of fruit and one present. By today's standards we were poor and had little. But back then, we appreciated what we had and didn't insist on more.

A black couple named Tom and Mary Hughs, our closest neighbors, had a small farm next to ours. Their house sat on a hill about a mile away. They didn't have any children, so they adopted us as their own. We called them Uncle Tom and Aunt Mary. This had nothing to do with the derogatory term "Uncle Tom" or the novel *Uncle Tom's Cabin* or the attitude that black people were subordinate in society. We simply loved Tom and Mary like family, and they loved us. We saw them as good people trying to scratch a living from the land just like us. Because of them, I never felt that black people were inferior to whites.

During my first trip to Nashville, Mom and I took the bus from Bellevue to downtown. I noticed that all the black passengers sat at the back end of the bus.

I asked Mom, "Why are all the black folks sitting in the back?"

Unprepared for this question and embarrassed about the Southern social norms of those times, she gave a quick answer to close the subject and talk about something else. This was my first experience with segregation. I didn't know that society relegated the good black people of our communities to second-class citizens. I thought of Uncle Tom and Aunt Mary. I thought of what wonderful neighbors they were and how much I loved them. None of this made sense to me.

To my recollection, Bellevue had two country stores about five miles apart. One store was by the railroad tracks, the other sat on the opposite side of this unincorporated community near our family farm. One of these stores contained the post office. State Highways 70 and 100 ran through Bellevue. Also, the Harpeth River flowed through our community. The main roads were paved, but the side roads were dirt. We didn't have any city services out there, no fire department, no ambulance, no city water or sewer. Bellevue had a small Baptist church, a Church of Christ, and a Methodist church, which had the largest congregation in the community.

I think two thousand people or so lived in Bellevue then. Consequently, everybody knew everybody. You couldn't get away with anything dubious because everybody knew you. Even though most people didn't have telephones in those days, if I got in trouble at school, my parents knew about it before I got home. I didn't know how but they knew. (To this day, I still haven't figured that one out.) If I received a spanking at school, I also got one when I arrived home.

All in all, Bellevue was a good community and a good place to grow up. People took care of people. People helped you but only if you worked hard yourself to make ends meet. America lost that sense of closeness within community. When we had funerals back then, scores of people attended. Families, friends, neighbors, and even children gathered to honor the deceased. (When I preside over funerals today, it's not uncommon for barely twenty people to attend.) Also noteworthy, back then people tried to solve their problems themselves. If a family had a problem, they first kept it to themselves and tried to work things out privately. (Nowadays, the first thing they do is post it to Facebook for all the world to see.)

Bellevue had one school for first through eighth grade called Harpeth Valley School, a single-story brick building sitting on about five acres of land. The teachers who worked there had done so for years. Each grade had one classroom and about twenty students. A total of about one hundred sixty children attended school there. A big room which had long tables and benches that folded down from the walls served as the lunch room and auditorium.

While in elementary school, I was scrawny for my age. I also mispronounced words and stuttered. Because of that, I went to speech class along with about five other students in the school. Other kids made fun of me because of the way I talked. I didn't believe they were malicious but simply amused themselves at my expense. They asked me to say something that they knew I would pronounce wrong and then laughed about it. I went along with it because I considered them my friends. It didn't really bother me. One day about the sixth or seventh grade, I simply outgrew these speech problems and began talking normally.

I had a group of kids that I hung out with on a regular basis: Tommy, Emery, Don, and my cousin Larry. We lived in the same general vicinity at one end of Bellevue. We did stuff together, went fishing a lot, but never did anything out of the ordinary, except for me and my cousin Larry. He worked for Mr. McClain who owned the country store that sat about five miles from my house if you walked the paved roads. Cutting through the woods always got you there quicker. Mr. McClain had Larry clean up the store each afternoon. He paid Larry twenty-five cents a day to sweep the floor to control the dust and take out the trash. Larry wanted me to hang out with him while he worked at the general store. When he finished, we went off to play.

One day, we got to thinking. While Larry worked, I could sneak behind the sales counter and steal a pack of cigarettes. We were about twelve years old. So, from time to time, I stole a pack of cigarettes while Larry swept and took out the trash. We smuggled the cigarettes down to the creek and hid them in a pipe. Occasionally, we ventured down to the creek and smoked cigarettes. A foolish thing to do, but it made us feel like big somebodies getting away with something crafty.

Years later, I wondered if maybe Mr. McClain knew that we stole packs of cigarettes. Back then they only cost a dime a pack, which was nothing to Mr. McClain. Everybody back then smoked. Nobody knew of the medical consequences. Perhaps people didn't care if we smoked a cigarette every now and then. We all knew of the Marlboro man and wanted to be tough like him. So, we stole that brand, Marlboros. We felt like we had really gotten away with something big.

Larry and I also liked to aggravate the truck drivers that drove down Highway 100. Back then the truckers used Highway 100 because we didn't have the interstate yet. Larry lived on that highway. When we wanted to have some fun, we hung around the road at night in the summer and waited for the big trucks to go by. When they did, we picked up handfuls of fine gravel from the side of the road and threw them into the air toward the trucks. When the gravel hit the metal cabs, it sounded like rifle shots going off. *Pow, pow, pow!* We had a good laugh as we startled the truck drivers who slowed down to figure out what just happened.

One night, though, when Larry and I did this, the truck driver locked up the brakes of his truck and came to a screeching halt right in the middle of Highway 100, the trailer swerving back and forth. Before we could fully grasp what happened, the trucker bolted out of the cab and started firing a pistol. *Bang, bang, bang!* Larry and I took off running.

I thought, "Man, he's trying to kill us!" I learned that night how hard it was to run with your heart lodged in your throat. That episode ended our gravel-throwing shenanigans. We never did that anymore!

We did things like this because we lived out in the country and had to find creative ways to entertain ourselves. Children in town probably played with pinball machines and such. We didn't have any of that out in Bellevue. All things considered, living in the country like that was a good way to grow up. We appreciated what we had and showed respect to our elders.

If I spoke to an adult without saying, "Yes, sir. Yes, ma'am," Daddy whipped me in front of them. Back then children honored and respected elders, a universal rule that died over the years, a very tragic thing.

When I started going to school and made friends, I left the family farm more often. I discovered that not everyone lived like we did. Other children had fathers with good-paying jobs in addition to farming. They had nice modern houses for the period of the 1950s. My friend Tommy had a daddy who made good money driving a tanker truck. They had a nice home. I went over to Tommy's house a lot and spent the night on occasion. Having become ashamed of the old farmhouse that I lived in, I never invited Tommy over. I never had any of my friends to the house.

One time when I was nine or ten years old, I spent Friday night at Tommy's house. His mom served spaghetti with French bread. That was the first time that I ever heard of spaghetti. At my house we usually had meat, beans, and potatoes. If we wanted to change it up a little then we had potatoes, beans, and meat. I thought that spaghetti dinner at Tommy's was the best meal ever. Because I never experienced such a dinner, I didn't know what I was missing.

I was content with my life until I got a little older and saw how other people lived better than we did. At that time in my childhood, I developed the desire to have more than what life simply handed to me. I had no idea how I would achieve this. I had little faith that I would ever rise above the lifestyle that I grew up in. At that time, I just didn't know how. Regardless, I determined in my heart that if I ever improved my standard of living, I would never go back to being poor.

One time, Mom took me with her to Nashville for the day. We went to Krystal for lunch.

When we walked up to the counter, a man asked, "What can I get you?"

Mom ordered, "I'll take a cheeseburger and fries."

Then the man asked, "Sonny, what would you like?"

I replied, "I don't know. These burgers are so small. I don't think they will fill me up. I don't know how many to order. I could probably eat the twelve-pack."

The man at the counter said, "Well, sonny, if you eat the entire twelve-pack, I'll pay for both your meals."

The challenge was on! We sat down at the counter and I ate the first four with no problem. Then I ate the next four quite easily. As I continued to eat, the burgers began to feel like bricks grinding against each other in my stomach. I struggled through the last four but finally ate all twelve burgers. Mom and I got a free meal that day from Krystal!

In fifth grade when I was about eleven years old, we had a bully in school named Jimmy, who in fact was my neighbor. His house sat about two miles from mine on the other side of a hill. He went about finding reasons to whip everybody in school. In those days, Rocky Marciano had been the heavyweight boxing champion of the world. Jimmy brought a pair of his daddy's work gloves to school and wore them as boxing gloves. As he beat up other boys, he pretended to be Rocky Marciano.

Hearing of all this, my brother Linton told me, "If you let Jimmy whip you, then I'm going to whip you also when you get home. So, make your mind up to stand your ground and don't let him beat you up."

I didn't know if Linton genuinely meant to look out for me or if he wanted a reason to whip me himself.

Soon after, on the school playground, we played softball during recess. Jimmy pitched that day. Scrawny in stature, I stood in the batter's box. Jimmy threw the ball over my head. I didn't swing.

Jimmy then said with a grin, "If you don't swing at this next pitch, I'm coming in to whip you!" He threw the next ball. It soared above my head. Again, I didn't swing. Jimmy hollered, "I'm giving you one more chance! If you don't swing at this one, I'm coming in to whip you!" He catapulted the final pitch over my head. I stood motionless.

Well, Jimmy started toward home plate putting on the work gloves. As he approached, he miscalculated a few things about the situation. Number one, I was scared to death. Number two, I had a baseball bat in my hands. Number three, Linton's ultimatum echoed in my ears. When Jimmy reached home plate, I swung the bat as hard as I could, hitting him across the head. I knocked him out cold, blood flying everywhere, children yelling frantically, teachers arriving on the scene in a panic. Back then, we didn't have ambulance service in the country. They put Jimmy in a car and took him to the hospital. I didn't know how badly I hurt him.

When I got home that evening, I told Linton what happened. Pleasantly surprised, almost incredulous, he gave me a high five. Linton was very excited that scrawny little me stood up for myself. I was excited that Linton wasn't going to beat me up. This experience taught me at an early age to confront bullies. Size and stature didn't matter. People needed to stand up for themselves and for what they believed in.

The next day at school, the loud speaker bellowed, "Herbie Mays, report to the principal's office."

Gossipy whispers echoed through the classroom as my fellow students speculated my fate. I figured that the principal would take the paddle to me. Uncertain of the immediate future, I slowly walked to the main office. I did not want to go. If I had a way to disappear or suddenly be somewhere else, I would have taken it. But there I remained in the quiet, empty hallway, steadily making my way to the principal's office, the sound of each step echoing off the still walls.

As I entered the main office, the secretary sternly said, "Herbie, take a seat. The principal will see you in a minute."

I sat there in a fog of nervous apprehension. A short while later, the principal called me to come in. I stood in front of his desk, my heart pounding loudly in my ears, my blood racing so fast that I could hardly breath.

The principal said, "Herbie, I want to tell you that Jimmy will be okay. He is going to stay at the hospital another day, but he will be fine." The principal continued. "Herbie, I want to tell you something, young man."

My heart stopped. I stood in a sea of dead silence.

After a tormenting pause with the principal glaring at me, he concluded with a smirk, "I have been waiting all year for someone to stand up to Jimmy and take care of him. Now get back to your class and continue with your schoolwork."

Swept away by surreal disbelief at what just happened, I returned to my classroom with a glowing smile on my face, a skip in my step, and tremendous joy in my heart. Everyone expected me to get a whipping and couldn't believe what the principal told me. After that confrontation, Jimmy and I became good friends all the way through high school. He acted as meek as a lamb from then on. Jimmy's family never got mad at me or my family because of that incident. Back then, people didn't begrudge those who stood up for themselves. Rather, they respected them.

When I was about twelve years old, Linton began working as a brick layer and made decent money for back then. On Friday nights, he came home with a case of beer and drank all weekend. By late Friday night, alcohol changed Linton from confrontational to extremely generous. Like many who got drunk, Linton gave the shirt off his back.

Because of this, I waited until he got good and drunk and then asked, "Hey, Linton, do you think I could have a dollar?"

He replied gleefully, "Sure! Just go in and get my billfold and take whatever you want."

So, every Friday night, I got a dollar from Linton. That dollar bought me ice cream at school every day for the week. I also walked to the country store and got a coke and a piece of candy for a nickel a piece. That dollar from Linton on Friday gave me a good week every week!

After Daddy phased out of farming, my youngest sister and I rode the bus to school in the morning. After school, my cousins, my sister, and I stopped in to visit my grandmother (my mom's mother) as we walked past her home. We called her Ma Lincoln. Then we went on to my uncle's house. Mom picked us up on her way home from work. By this time, Mom had a steady job and bought her own car. When my youngest sister and I got home in the late afternoon/ early evening, we cleaned the house for Mom.

Ma Lincoln emerged as one of the greatest influences in my life. Her genuine love for and positive confession over me during my younger days greatly shaped the man I became. A full-blooded Cherokee Indian, she had coal black hair that she always kept in a bun. I remember Ma Lincoln's dark black hair even into her old age. Small in stature and a bit frail, she probably didn't even weigh ninety pounds. Her great grandparents or so had come from Cherokee, North Carolina on the trail of tears. They didn't go all the way to Oklahoma, but settled in Fairview, Tennessee right outside of Bellevue. My grandfather earned a living as a blacksmith. I never knew him because he died before I was born.

Ma Lincoln usually had freshly baked biscuits from the wood stove that she shared with us when we stopped by. However, some days she didn't have enough to go around. In those instances, she visited with all of us for a while and then sent the other children off to play. After they left, she took out the few biscuits she had and share them with me. Because of this and because she continually encouraged me, I felt that maybe she favored me most, although I knew that she loved all her grandchildren dearly.

A devoted Methodist, Ma Lincoln always refer to her Bible as her *Methodist* Bible even though it was the same Bible we had as Baptists. I don't ever remember her getting mad or upset about anything, always a mild, little lady. She suffered from arthritis due to years of hard work and raising thirteen children. She had trouble walking and couldn't go to church.

Ma Lincoln lived in a one-room apartment with no running water, an old wood stove, and scant electrical lighting. The apartment building was a renovated old country store. I don't think she even paid five dollars a month to live there. She collected about fifty dollars a month in social security benefits as a widow. In addition, her children met her needs even though Ma Lincoln didn't desire or require much. She learned contentment with basic food, clothing, and shelter. Something not seen much today.

When I stopped by to visit, Ma Lincoln always read me a scripture, encouraged me, and gave me something to eat.

She told me, "Herbie, God is going to use you and do great things through your life. You are going to do great things."

I didn't fully grasp the meaning of her words at the time. Because of my humble beginnings, I never visualized doing something noteworthy or ever having anything. However, my grandmother put so much positive influence into me with her encouraging words during those early years of my life. For some reason, she had absolute faith in this stuttering, scrawny boy ridiculed by others. Perhaps she had a grandma's sixth sense about me. Maybe God spoke to her somehow. I didn't know. However, because of her influence, I dared to reach for the stars when I got older. If God believed in me enough to use me as she said He would, and if my grandmother had that much faith in me, then I could, at least, dare to believe in myself and try to achieve beyond my station in life.

Ma Lincoln knew that praying and confessing positive things over children and grandchildren produced powerful results. She had lots of time on her hands and spent much of it praying for her grandchildren. She read the Bible and prayed throughout the day. Her prayers and positive confession over me girded me for the things that God intended to do with my life. Whether she knew it or not, this amazing, uneducated Cherokee woman prophesied how God would have His hand upon me in the decades to come, how God would forge a remarkable journey out of my life.

I was twelve years old the night that Ma Lincoln died. My mom, Aunt Rosetta, and I were at my grandmother's home with her. By this time, Aunt Rosetta and Uncle Clifton converted their detached garage into an apartment and moved Ma Lincoln there so she could live closer to them. In her eighties at that time, she laid bedridden and sickly. Despite her condition, she slept peacefully waiting for that inevitable moment. When it arrived, she stopped breathing, and her spirit departed.

One of the darkest times I've ever known, I lost the only person who genuinely believed that I could do spectacular things with my life. Ma Lincoln was the only person that I could comfortably talk to about anything. She embodied unconditional love. I experienced no criticism or judgement at her hand. That night, my world crumbled. Ma Lincoln's love and encouragement meant more to me than words could ever express.

CHAPTER 3

Ups and Downs

When I was thirteen, fourteen, and fifteen, I traveled to Wilmington, North Carolina to spend the summer with my oldest sister, Joann, and her husband. His family owned a large peanut farm and a gas station with a repair shop. I spent the summer working in the repair shop sweeping, cleaning up, and changing oil in vehicles. I earned a few dollars a day. These trips forged a closeness between me and Joann that lasted to today.

Looking back, my parents instilled in me the value and importance of honest work. We worked on the farm as young children. When we got older, we had to earn money if we wanted to buy things. One time, I wanted to buy a bicycle from Mr. McClain at the general store. He had it on sale for twenty-five dollars.

Mr. McClain knew our family well and said to me, "Herbie, go ahead and take the bicycle. When you get the money, you can pay me."

So, I went home and told Daddy, "Mr. McClain said that I could have that bicycle and just pay him whenever I get the money."

Daddy retorted, "No, you are not going to do that. You are not getting anything until you pay for it. You will have to work until you earn enough money to buy it."

I got a job that summer working for a dollar a day in the hay fields. I worked thirty days for my oldest brother who had a custom hay baling business at the time. Mr. Herndon bought the equipment for him to start his own business, and my brother paid him back. This showed how people helped others who were willing to work hard to earn an honest living. My brother threw the hay bales up onto the trailer as I drove the tractor. We left out at dawn and didn't stop until dusk. The hot sun beat down on us all day. Even though it was hard work, I enjoyed it.

If we worked on a farm near the general store, we came in and bought some food. If not, we brought food with us for the day. We didn't have coolers in those days, so we wrapped paper around gallon jugs to keep our water somewhat cool. I raised the money and bought my bicycle. I learned this lesson at a young age. If you wanted anything in this world, then you must work for it. Nothing was free. Learning this helped me through the military, to stick with it, to work hard, and to achieve something.

When I was fourteen, I earned money digging trenches for the metro water department, which began to install city water in Bellevue. I got paid fifty cents a foot to dig a ditch from Highway 100 to the houses along that road. It only took me a few days to dig a trench for a single house using a shovel and pick. With this job, I raised the money to buy a steer to show at competitions and fairs because I participated in Future Farmers of America (FFA).

One day that fall, the agricultural teacher took me to Mr. Doubleday's farm after school so I could buy the steer. We picked one out. Unfortunately, Mr. Doubleday wanted one hundred fifty dollars for it.

I replied, "Sir, I only have one hundred dollars."

Mr. Doubleday said, "Well go ahead and take it. You can pay me the fifty dollars when you get it."

I took the calf home and trained it for showing. I never entered that steer in any competition because my parents divorced, and I moved to the city. A couple years later, Mr. Doubleday passed away. I never paid him the fifty dollars that I owed him. That bothered me. Daddy was right. I shouldn't have taken the steer without fully paying for it.

Years later, after I got saved, this bothered me so much that I gave an extra fifty dollars into the church offering to make up for it. I felt good for a little while. Then sometime later, it bothered me again.

Giving another fifty dollars, I pleaded, "Lord, forgive me for not paying Mr. Doubleday the money I owed him." I did this numerous times over the years because I just couldn't forgive myself.

Finally, I felt like the Lord dealt with me by saying in a silent voice, "How many times are you going to pay this fifty dollars back?"

God reminded me that Mr. Doubleday owned Doubleday Coal Company in Nashville. The fifty dollars was nothing to him. He had a beautiful farm with black angus cattle. He needed the fifty dollars like he needed a hole in the head. I finally forgave myself and realized that God forgave me for it a long time ago when the blood of Jesus washed me of my sins. God had thrown this indiscretion into the sea of forgottenness. I was the one bringing it up all these years.

In 1960, I enjoyed living in the country. I enjoyed going to school and participating in FFA. My family earned a modest living but wanted for nothing. Suddenly, my world capsized. After about twenty-five years of marriage, my parents divorced. Even though I went to church regularly, I didn't have a personal relationship with God at the time. The only institutions that I had faith in, marriage and the family, just collapsed. After the divorce, I lived with Mom for two years because Daddy didn't want me. For those who are unloved by a parent, I learned later in life that there is a God in Heaven Who wants to be your Loving Daddy. Deuteronomy 31:6 and Hebrews 13:5 tell us that if we embrace God as our Loving Daddy, then He will never leave us nor forsake us.

Mom had a decent job and owned her own car. Looking back, I concluded that she just got tired of Daddy and his attitude. I wondered if that marriage ever made her happy. Coming of age in a small farming community during the Great Depression of the 1930s, she didn't have much of a choice in selecting a husband. If a woman wanted to get married then, she selected the most eligible man in the vicinity and went for it.

My parents never enjoyed each other's company, no joyful talks, no sitting together on the couch, nothing. Daddy did his thing and Mom did hers. They coexisted in the same house and family. They didn't have love in their marriage and simply tolerated each other. Although they never had any big fights, they didn't enjoy being with each other. I didn't remember Daddy ever kissing or hugging Mom.

Mr. Herndon bought our seventy-two-acre farm for ten thousand dollars. After Daddy split the proceeds with Mom, she moved to Nashville, while Daddy continued to live in the old family house until he died. Mr. Herndon arranged a job for Daddy with Clements Paper Company in Nashville. Daddy completely quit farming at that time. Before the divorce, Mom, my younger sister, and I seemed one family. Daddy and the two older boys seemed another. (Joann lived in North Carolina by this time.) After the divorce, we indeed became two distinct families. Daddy and my brothers totally disowned me.

As a country boy now living in the city, my enthusiasm for school evaporated, my attendance sporadic. Lost in a fog of disillusion, I dropped out of school and left home at the age of sixteen. I lived with family and friends, drifting from one home to the next, never staying long anywhere. I took employment wherever I could find it, hitchhiking back and forth between Bellevue and Nashville as needed. I did construction work in the city and farm work in the country for five dollars a day. I considered it a very vagabond existence. When I earned enough money, I went to the bus station in Nashville and bought a ticket to somewhere. I made trips to Texas, Mississippi, and Oklahoma.

One time I went to Wichita Falls, Texas because I wanted to work on a ranch. I heard that Texas had ranches. I stayed at a motel for a week or two. The rooms cost only about five dollars a day. I watched television, did some sightseeing, and sought adventure. Not finding ranch work or adventure, I returned to Nashville. I also went to Senatobia, Mississippi because I heard of a big ranch out there. For my last trip, I went to Tulsa, Oklahoma. Little did I know that God would later bring me back here for a greater purpose. As a sixteen-year-old on my own in the early 1960s, no one bothered me on these trips. I met very nice people. They asked me my story and sometimes treated me to a meal.

CHAPTER 4

Careful What You Ask For

On September 18, 1964, I turned eighteen years old. On that date, I walked to the highway and hitchhiked to downtown Nashville with the intention of joining the armed forces. I figured that I could succeed at serving in the military. It would get me out of town and be steady work. Also, perhaps I could see the world. I eagerly walked into the naval recruiting office which promptly turned me away because I didn't have a high school diploma. Disappointed but not deterred, I walked over to the air force recruiting office only to experience the same fate. I quickly realized the value of education and the opportunities it provided.

My disappointment turned into dejection. Determined not to give up, I walked into the army recruiting office with a glimmer of hope still flickering within me. To my joy, the army at that time took just about anyone.

I told the army recruiters, "I don't want a desk job. I want the toughest thing that the army has."

They set me up to go into the infantry and attend airborne school. By two o'clock that afternoon, I took my physical along with a bunch of draftees who had reported for duty in the army.

The joy of joining the army was short-lived. A few weeks later I stepped onto Fort Polk, Louisiana for basic training.

I thought, "What in the world did I get myself into!"

I was one of the few regular army enlistees in a sea of draftees. All of us striving to get through basic training. Fort Polk was called the h—hole of the South and for good reason. Terribly hot and muggy, it had mosquitos as big as a coffee cup. Back then the three-story wooden barracks didn't have air conditioning. We only had big fans to blow the hot air around. I found it very hard to sleep at night.

One of the first things they did was give us dozens of shots in each arm with an air-gun-type syringe. If a soldier was not careful and moved during a shot, he would end up bleeding everywhere. Next, we filed through the barber shop.

As I sat down in the barber chair, the barber asked, "How would you like to have your hair cut?"

I replied, "Just a little trim please."

The next thing I knew, I was bald. Guys cussed out the barbers right and left.

The drill sergeants back then used salty language. My drill sergeant was an older guy, probably with fifteen years of service or so. He probably fought in the Korean War, but I didn't know that for sure. One day, he got fed up with one of the draftees, who constantly mouthed off. At the end of the training day, we assembled back in our barracks on the third floor. The sun had just gone down and night set in. The drill sergeant came in and told that draftee that he needed to see him outside.

We figured that something was going to happen, so we all ran to the windows to see. The drill sergeant, the physically smaller man of the two, took the draftee outside and proceeded to whip this guy like a dog. We all pressed at the windows watching the whole thing. The drill sergeant brought him back in, standing the guy before us all beaten and bloody.

The drill sergeant asked us, "Did anyone see anything?"

We all replied, "No, Drill Sergeant! We didn't see a thing!"

After that, nobody caused any problems for the drill sergeants. We were what they called a strac unit, top-notch.

We got up early in the morning and did physical training (PT). Then we went to breakfast. Afterward we spent the day doing weapons training at the rifle or grenade range or trained with our masks in the gas chamber. Sometimes we did classroom-type training.

After basic training, I did my advance training as an infantry soldier there at Fort Polk as well. The toughest thing I remember doing was the twenty-eight-and-a-half-mile march in full combat gear. In that heat, soldiers dropped like flies. It was the roughest thing that I ever did during my training. Upon graduating, many of the guys went to Germany, some to Korea, and the rest went all over the USA. I went to Fort Benning, Georgia to attend airborne school. However, I injured my ankle the first week and dropped from the course. From then on, I was a regular ground pounder in the infantry. At that point, I got orders to go to Korea.

When I joined up, the only thing I knew about the army was that they had a base in Kentucky north of Nashville, Tennessee called Fort Campbell. I didn't know where troops were stationed around the world or that we were in a war. When I got my orders to go to Korea, I didn't even know where Korea was. I traveled across the Pacific Ocean on a troop ship for about three weeks of misery. The army didn't give out Dramamine. I lived on saltine crackers and 7-Up. Some days I started to feel better and made my way to the mess hall. As I got close enough to smell the food, seasickness rushed over me like a big wave knocking me down at the beach. The misery engulfed me again.

During the day, we didn't have much to do. We played cards, went up on deck, and just sat around. The bunks we slept in lined the wall four rows high, with two feet or so of space between them vertically. Stacked on the floor next to our bunks, our duffle bags held what little belongings we had. Boredom and sickness owned me.

Upon arriving, I spent thirteen months in Korea. I reported for duty at a place called Taejon about four hours south of Seoul, the capital city. As one of the larger cities, Taejon sat inland a bit from the Yellow Sea. The railroad made Taejon a major transportation hub for the country. (Today, this city is called Daejeon.) Korea had changing seasons, hot in the summer and cold in the winter. Forests and low brush covered the hilly, mountainous terrain. Lowlands ran along the west coast and major rivers. Korea had no thick jungles.

We guarded an ammo depot where the army positioned munitions for the war in Vietnam. The ammunition shipped from the US to Korea and then to Vietnam. In Korea, I heard for the first time about Vietnam and the war to stop the spread of communism. Surprised that we fought a war in Vietnam, I wanted to go. As an infantryman who had not seen any action so far, only guard duty, I didn't fear going to war. We were in the army and were at war, so let's go. These were my sentiments on the matter.

I would eventually learn one of life's important lessons: "Be careful what you ask for. You just might get it."

Each day, we got up early for PT and would run up what we called Taejon hill. Our camp nestled in a valley with Taejon on the other side of this hill. After PT, we had breakfast and then reported for duty guarding the ammo depot. We ran three eight-hour shifts. Sometimes I would have the day shift, sometimes the evening shift, and sometimes the midnight shift.

We spent eight hours in a guard tower by ourselves, very boring duty. In the central guard tower in the middle of the compound we had four soldiers and an M60 machinegun, less cumbersome duty. Eight individual towers extending about thirty feet in the air lined the perimeter and overlooked the compound. At that point in history, Korea had no action at all. Earning my general education degree and making the rank of specialist made the top of the list of the most exciting things that happened to me there.

A company-size unit, we lived in a little compound of about three to four hundred people. It had a post exchange, snack bar, and a USO (United Service Organizations) club. I got to know a lot of people pretty well. I had a friend named Warren. We would get a three-day pass and catch a train to Seoul about once a month. Seoul had movie theaters, restaurants, bars, and nice hotels, a very modern city in the 1960s.

My thirteen uneventful months in Korea came to an end. As I prepared to return to the US, I didn't have enough room in my travel box for my eight-track tape player. (Anyone remember those?) I had taken it to the USO club and recorded all kinds of music on it.

I told Warren, "I have to sell the eight-track tape player because I can't take it with me."

He asked me, "How much do you want for it?"

I told him, "Fifty dollars."

Warren suggested, "I don't have fifty dollars right now, but if you let me have the player, I will send the money to your home address once I get paid."

Since I was going home on leave after Korea, I agreed. While home, I never received the money. While at my next duty station, I never received the money nor heard from Warren. I concluded that I would never see him, the eight-track tape player, or the money ever.

I came back to the US in April 1966. The army stationed me at Fort Lewis, Washington with the Fourth Infantry Division, which the army filled mostly with draftees in preparation for Vietnam. A vast evergreen forest sat upon the mountainous terrain in Washington State. It rained a lot in the northwest. Mount Rainier could be seen off in the distance. It rained most of the time in the state of Washington. An extremely cold winter lingered over us that year. Did I mention that it rained a lot there? We lived in two-story wooden barracks without air conditioning or central heat.

I worked in the company headquarters of A Company, Second Battalion, Twenty-Second Infantry Regiment, Third Brigade doing training schedules with a sergeant. After a month, the sergeant left the unit. I scheduled the company training by myself from then on, so the commander promoted me to sergeant as the training NCO (noncommissioned officer). Surprised by my promotion, I felt good about myself and life, a sergeant at the age of nineteen. After another month, the commander sent me to the country of Panama to attend a school run by the Jungle Operations Training Center located at Fort Sherman in the Panama Canal Zone to learn jungle warfare and guerilla fighting.

Jungle warfare school lasted a few weeks in a thick tropical rainforest. Special Forces instructors constantly kept us on the go twenty-four hours a day, seven days a week. We got very little sleep. The course trained us intensely on how to travel and survive the jungle, find and disarm booby traps, and escape and evade capture. Because the training, terrain, and climate were highly unpleasant, I decided that I never wanted to come back to Panama ever again.

I declared, "I will never come back to this godforsaken place again!" Little did I know.

After my training there, I returned to Fort Lewis, Washington. I was a jungle warfare instructor with the Fourth Infantry Division. Four other soldiers and I spent two months teaching platoons in the division the basics of guerrilla warfare and jungle fighting. We spent a day teaching a different platoon important jungle warfare topics like booby traps and to secure your grenades with duct tape so the pin didn't accidently pull out while going through the jungle. For the most part, the draftees were good students even though they were upset having been ordered away from their families. They knew that war awaited them, so they took the training seriously.

The Fourth Infantry Division poised to ship out to Vietnam. In 1965 and 1966, the US built up the military strength over there. In it's heyday, we had over five hundred thousand troops in Vietnam. I didn't have to go because I only had thirteen months left in the service. I could have stayed back at Fort Lewis for the remainder of my enlistment. But I volunteered to go. I wanted to go to Vietnam. As a result, I became a squad leader responsible for fifteen soldiers in First Platoon of Alpha Company of the Triple Deuce (Second Battalion/Twenty-Second Infantry Regiment).

A nineteen-year-old squad leader in the army, I had draftee squad members two to four years older than me. I had a specialist named David Berkholz as one of my team leaders. He was a twenty-one-year-old draftee from Michigan. He rose to the rank of specialist quickly because he was an above-average guy. As time went by, David became my best friend.

I also had Specialist Bill Sealy, a tall muscular black guy from the Midwest. He had an opportunity to try out for the Cleveland Browns football team but got drafted by the military instead. He chose to honor the draft and serve in the army. He put his life on hold and in danger to serve his country. Bill joined our unit after we arrived in Vietnam. Bill always helped in any situation. We could always depend on him. We made him an M60 machine-gunner because he was big and strong and could carry the larger weapon more easily than most.

Our company commander, Captain Ken Both, earned his commission at Officer Candidate School (OCS). The army referred to him as a *mustang* because he served as an enlisted soldier before becoming an officer. He was competent, compassionate, and caring—what we called a strac soldier—professional, squared away, and reliable. We had great respect for him.

The night before we left for Vietnam, I gathered my squad and told them, "It is my job to get all of you back. I don't plan on leaving any of you behind."

We were told to get with our squads and tell them that some of them weren't coming back, a reality check. In my heart, I just couldn't accept that. In September of 1966, we shipped out from Tacoma, Washington on the USNS General Nelson M. Walker.

I spent another miserable three weeks or so devoured by sickness and boredom as we crossed the Pacific Ocean. Once again, my diet consisted of saltine crackers and 7-Up. We bunked in the lower section of the ship, the air very stuffy and hot down there. People getting sick made the atmosphere even worse. We constantly mopped up messes. It was awful! On September 18, 1966, I had my twentieth birthday at sea. Needless to say, I didn't eat birthday cake.

I believe each company bunked in its own huge room with rows and rows of bunks stacked four high with about two feet of room between each vertically. If you raised up in the bunk, you might touch the bunk above you. Narrow walkways separated the rows of bunks. We got some relief up on deck where we could enjoy the cool ocean breeze and fresh air. I also got a temporary reprieve from sickness at night when I slept and for a few days when we stopped in Guam.

Every now and then, we received a class on something pertaining to the war, such as how to treat the civilians to win over their hearts and minds. On the ship, reality started to set in that war awaited us. Some of us would not come back, maybe even me. Regardless, as soldiers, we would fight this war. At the time, we knew of the war protesters but didn't pay much attention to them. Back then, we didn't watch much TV anyway. After we got to Vietnam, we lived isolated from the rest of the world.

We arrived at Vung Tau, Vietnam on October 9, 1966 but didn't disembark until October 12. Terribly weakened, I could hardly carry my belongings. Trucks transported us to a secure area for a few weeks of training, orientation, and adapting to the new terrain and climate, which felt like one hundred twenty degrees during the day with constant high humidity. In this *safe and secure* area, I tasted the horrors of the Vietnam War for the first time. We sat down to eat lunch one day along a fence line at the edge of the jungle. We got C rations for breakfast and lunch and a hot meal for dinner.

We sat about three feet apart from each other in a long line. We had little gasoline stoves to heat up the C rations. As I heated my food, a sniper shot a soldier about six feet from me. Shot in the head, he died instantly. A second sniper round hit my stove, causing it to blow up and catch me on fire. My uniform from the waist up burnt onto my body, causing second and third-degree burns. My fellow soldiers smothered the flames by rolling me on the ground for a minute or so. At this point, I realized that the war in Vietnam was very real with no safe place to rest. This experience taught me vigilance and to never take anything for granted.

They medevacked me by helicopter to a burn unit in a hospital where I spent the next two weeks getting treatment for my wounds. The intense pain tormented me. After three or four days though, I started feeling better, only sore rather than painful. The doctors said that the burns would scar me for life. I felt miserable. I had seen pictures of burn victims and felt I would be a mutilated sight that everyone would stare at.

I thought about everything that I went through the past six months. I attended a challenging jungle training course, spent weeks sick crossing the Pacific Ocean, and now burnt from the waist up, might be put out of the war. This was a lot for a twenty-year-old to endure in a short period of time. I wondered if it may be for the best. Not as tough as I had thought I was, I had enough of war and its tragedies.

After a few weeks, a nurse removed the bandages and stared in disbelief. She ran off calling for the doctor. I thought that something had gone terribly wrong. The doctor came in and looked in amazement. Miraculously, I had all new skin with no scarring whatsoever. The doctors found it hard to believe that my skin regenerated like it did in such a short period of time. They kept bringing people to me to show them my skin. Extremely shocked but pleased at my unmarred appearance, I started believing that I just may get out of this h—hole alive. I simply felt that way inside. Something protected me, even in this place, and I would survive the war.

I returned to my unit and accompanied it to our new home, the Dau Tieng Base Camp located about fifty miles north of Saigon, the capital city of South Vietnam. For half the month of December, our company filled and placed sandbags to build up the base's defenses. The perimeter of the camp was protected by an earthen berm, sand bags, and triple-strand concertina wire with empty cans hanging from it to make noise. Claymore mines were placed around the perimeter as well. It also had defensive bunkers to fight from.

We spent about thirty days at a time out in the bush conducting search and clear operations. At night, we circled the APCs and created a company defensive position. We posted guards and sent out an ambush patrol. We lived on three to five hours of sleep a night. When our time in the bush ended, we came into the base camp at evening. We spent the next day doing maintenance on our weapons, equipment, and vehicles. Usually the following day, we went back into the bush for another thirty days. We didn't spend much time in the base camp, which sat between the village of Dau Tieng and the Michelin rubber plantation.

The area had dense jungles with clearings of tall grass here and there. A lot of rivers ran through it as well. We liked to jump into the river to cool off because of the hot, thick, still air. Our jungle fatigues dried quickly. We willfully suffered the blood leaches to cool off. We used cigarettes to remove the leaches. It was worth it to us.

Out in the bush, we each carried an M16 assault rifle, a bayonet, four grenades, and about eighty rounds of ammunition. In addition, as squad leader, I had a .45-caliber pistol and a night vision scope.

The squad had two M60 machine guns and two grenade launchers and some machetes. If we ever got into a tight spot, I had to destroy the night vision scope so that the enemy wouldn't get it. It was a valuable piece of equipment and very expensive back then. We trained on the M14 rifle back in the US. In Vietnam, we received the M16 but never trained on it. Unfortunately for the US soldier, the M16 was a new weapon of which all the bugs were not yet worked out. Particularly, the M16 jammed regularly.

North Vietnamese regulars and the Vietcong would travel the Ho Chi Minh trail through Cambodia and cross into South Vietnam in this area. We had a lot of enemy activity. To counter this, we ran a lot of patrols. One of my main duties was to take two men and do LRRPs for two to four days at a time. We would search the jungles looking for the enemy. Between the three of us, we had a radio which we used to talk with the company headquarters. We cut our way through the jungle underbrush using a machete. We labored intensely hacking away at vines, branches, and razor-sharp tall grass, especially in that hot, heavy air. We struggled through the jungle constantly exhausted and drenched with sweat.

We usually only went a few miles a day when patrolling through the dense jungle. Looking for booby traps and punji pits slowed our progress, every step focused and deliberate. We purposely moved slowly. We never rushed ourselves. We took breaks and drank water to avoid heat sickness. If we ran low on water, we used water from springs or water falls and purified it with iodine tablets. We heard bird and monkey chatter while going through the jungle. If they got excited, we knew something was up. If the jungle got eerily quiet, we knew something was up. After a while, I developed a sense of danger.

We looked for enemy camps, for where they had been, or their current activity. When we came to a village, we got a feel for if the enemy had been there by how the villagers acted. Our main priority was to not be seen by the enemy. If our small patrol encountered the enemy, we would try to stay hidden and call in artillery. We did these patrols as reconnaissance, not search and clear missions. We did our best to move stealthily through the jungle, a tough thing to do when we had to hack our way through the underbrush. While I conducted

LRRPs, the remainder of my squad did operations with the rest of the platoon and company.

I also performed duty as a tunnel rat, clearing out tunnels that we found in the area. From Cu Chi up to Dau Tieng, the enemy had elaborate tunnel systems with underground barracks, mess halls, and medical clinics. Fortunately, our area only had simple tunnels that ran a couple hundred yards. The enemy used them to hide from us as we went by. When we found a tunnel, we threw smoke grenades in it and covered up the entrance to see where else the smoke came out. After the smoke cleared, another soldier and I went into the tunnel to search for the enemy.

Because the tunnel was so narrow, we had to crawl or duck walk single file through it with a bayonet in our mouth, a .45-caliber pistol in one hand, and a flashlight in the other. If we had room, we held the flashlight up and away from our head and body as we went through the tunnel. I usually took about an hour to clear a tunnel, greatly relieved to come out the other end. Fortunately, I only had to clear four or five tunnels, which were all empty. But some guys encountered the enemy, and it cost them their life. Clearing tunnels was an adrenaline-pumping, frightening experience.

The second instance in Vietnam where I got injured, I tripped on something in the jungle and fell into a small pit filled with punji sticks. The Vietcong dug holes in the ground, put sharpened bamboo sticks in it, smeared the spikes with feces to cause infection, and covered the pit with brush. A lot of soldiers got killed falling into these pits. When I fell into one, a punji stick went into my left knee. Fortunately, I didn't fall all the way in. I fell on the side of the pit where only one spike went into my leg. The medic cleaned and dressed my wound, and I spent a few days in the hospital. I then rejoined my unit. Not falling fully into the punji pit strengthened my conviction that, for some reason, I had some kind of protection over me.

By this time, I earned the respect of my squad members. A regular army enlistee with two years of military experience and jungle warfare training, I led by example. I never asked my soldiers to do anything that I wouldn't do. At times, I even took the point position when the squad patrolled. As a squad leader, I wasn't supposed to do this because the point position was the most dangerous. This soldier had the lead spot in front of the patrol and usually had the misfortune of stopping the first enemy bullet. Since I did things like this, my squad members listened to me.

Unfortunately, new soldiers who didn't know me ignored my advice, probably because of my young age.

One day, I told a replacement draftee, "Put duct tape around your grenades whenever you're out in the bush. This prevents the vegetation from accidently pulling out the pin and setting off the grenade."

We usually carried four grenades a piece. He didn't want to do this because he felt it would take too long to cut the tape off if he had to use the grenade. Two weeks later, he blew himself up while on patrol. Fortunately, no one else got hurt. I wish he had listened to me.

In December 1966, Captain Both recommended me, as well as a staff sergeant in the company, for a battlefield commission to the rank of second lieutenant. Our promotions would come through sometime in the spring. Extremely surprised, I decided to make the army my career. A country boy and high school dropout would go from the rank of private to second lieutenant in about two and a half years. Although young, I felt my hard work and dedication paid off.

Captain Both didn't put up with slack conduct, and neither did I. I led by example, and the draftees respected me for it. Because of this, I had one of the best squads in the unit. In war, survival instincts mattered more than education. I worked well with my platoon sergeant and platoon leader. I felt like the Fourth Infantry Division was a good outfit. My unit didn't have many disciplinary problems from my perspective. We did our job well.

One night, however, I foolishly jeopardized all this while on radio duty. We senior enlisted soldiers usually did radio duty because it was nice duty. We had that day off, did radio duty from six in the evening until six the next morning, and then had the rest of the second day off too. The headquarters tent sat next to the mess tent, so we ate well.

About midnight, I got this radio call that said, "Select two soldiers from your unit to go to Cu Chi tomorrow to see the Bob Hope Christmas show. Have them at the flight tarmac at zero six hundred hours to be picked up by a helicopter."

I hustled down to our squad's tent and told David to meet me at the tarmac at six o'clock because we were going to Cu Chi to see the Bob Hope show.

Having lived in the boonies for weeks, we would now soon see the Bob Hope show and get a good meal. Cu Chi had everything. I anticipated lots of fun. We arrived at Cu Chi about eight o'clock in the morning and had a great day! We saw the Bob Hope show, which had the Les Brown Band and movie stars like Anita Bryant, Phyllis Diller, and Joey Heatherton. Diane Shelton autographed my battle prayer card that I always kept with me for protection. We ate a good meal in the chow hall, a real treat after having mostly C rations for the last couple months.

That evening around five o'clock, we flew back to Dau Tieng. On the way back, a sinking feeling in the pit of my stomach replaced the joy and excitement. I started to realize that I was in big trouble. I didn't tell anyone where David and I went, so technically we were AWOL (absent without official leave) even though I had the day off following radio duty. We didn't have permission from the company commander to go to Cu Chi. I looked at David and told him that he would probably have rank on me after this because I figured that I would get busted to private. Toward the end of the flight, I concluded that I made a big mistake.

When we got back, a black cloud enshrouded me. I knew I deserved punishment but futilely hoped nothing would happen. Guilt and condemnation berated me.

After about an hour, one of the soldiers came to me and said, "Sergeant Mays, the captain wants to see you."

Grieved, I went to accept my fate and reported to Captain Both.

He asked, "Sergeant Mays, where have you been today?"

I had to tell him the truth. "David and I went down to Cu Chi to see the Bob Hope show. I got a call last night while on radio duty that two of our guys would be picked up by helicopter to go."

The captain said very sternly, "Do you know, Sergeant, that I could court-martial you into a private because you were AWOL!?" After an awkward pause, the captain continued. "The only thing that really makes me mad about this is that you didn't wake me up to go!" Captain Both then smirked.

At that point, I knew nothing would happen to me. We had a laugh about the whole thing. Perhaps the captain already knew where we went. I think he let me off the hook because I told him the truth and he was fond of me. The dark cloud evaporated like a huge weight lifted of my shoulders. Greatly relieved, I felt glad I had told Captain Both the truth.

Also, in December, I went to Hawaii for a three-day R & R (rest and recuperation). Vietnam time proceeded that of Hawaii by seventeen hours. I sort of traveled back in time during the six-hour flight. I left early on the first day and arrived in Hawaii the evening before if you go by dates. Of course, this didn't add any more time to my R & R. The three days off went according to Vietnam time only. Once in Hawaii, I walked around Waikiki Beach, did some sightseeing, and had an enjoyable time in an environment truly safe from bullets, grenades, mortars, and booby traps. Unfortunately, time marched forth undaunted, the inevitable moment arrived, and I returned to Vietnam.

I flew back on Braniff International which had the government contract to do the R & R flights. As the plane approached Tan Son Nhut Air Base near Saigon, dusk had just pushed the last bit of daylight over the edge of the Vietnam horizon. Suddenly, the pilot abruptly pulled out of the landing approach decent.

He announced over the intercom, "The airfield is receiving enemy ground fire. We're going to make another landing run."

I thought he would circle the airfield until he received the all clear from below. Instead, he circled once and then nosedived toward the front of the landing strip. Pulling up at the last second, he landed the plane using only a short stretch of the runway. I didn't think the plane even rolled a hundred feet on the ground. As the plan shimmied to a halt, it rocked vigorously back and forth.

The pilot spoke again over the intercom, "Sorry, folks, for the aggressive maneuver. It was necessary to avoid the ground fire. Thank you for flying our friendly skies."

Stunned and amazed at the same instant, I concluded that this civilian pilot definitely knew how to fly!

From time to time, my squad pulled twenty-four-hour guard duty at the water hole, a concrete-topped drilled well from which tanker trucks pumped water daily for the surrounding camps. It sat about a mile from our base camp. During one of these times, South Vietnamese civilians came by and offered to sell us boonie hats, a wide brim soft cap much more comfortable than the steel helmets we normally wore. Several of us bought one. We reveled in our comfort while performing guard duty in the boiling jungle heat.

Later that day, our lieutenant arrived to check on our status. When he saw us wearing the boonie hats, he had a fit. "Get those ———, ——— boonies off your head! Put your helmets back on! Those boonies aren't going to protect you from shrapnel! Give them all to me!"

As nineteen and twenty-year-old kids, we gave little regard to practicality. We sought to ease our plight and grimaced at the lieutenant who walked off with our two-dollar investments in comfort.

One day, the entire company maneuvered toward a certain road to set up an ambush. The enemy used that road to move supplies. As we passed through an open area, enemy sharpshooters ambushed us from a tree line on the edge of the jungle. Shooting at us from up in the trees, they wounded one of our soldiers in the leg. Since they had the jump on us, we pulled back about a half mile. Captain Both called in air support. Three or four jets came through and made two passes over the area where the enemy sharpshooters fired at us. I didn't know how many bombs the jets dropped, but the explosions of napalm shot white bursts of fumes into the air. Then a wave of heat hit us even though we were a half mile away. It felt like a big oven door had opened and smelled something like diesel. The company set up a defensive position there for the night.

The next morning, we went into the napalmed area, which stretched about a quarter mile long and an eighth of a mile wide.

All the foliage burned away. Just the stalks and main branches of the trees remained. The charred terrain had a nauseating ashy smell. Twenty feet up into the trees we saw the blackened bodies of the sharpshooters tied to branches, about ten of them. I don't know why they were tied to the trees so that they couldn't get away. I called them kamikaze or suicide snipers.

I thought to myself, "What an awful way to die!"

I think their job was to fight to the death and occupy our attention, while a larger force flanked us from behind. That didn't happen because we pulled back and called in air support. We then swept the area and didn't find the enemy. The company returned to base camp, never having set up the ambush. This was the only time I ever saw napalm used.

Decades later, I preached a sermon based on this experience titled "Recognize, Analyze, and Mobilize." When you encounter problems in life, you must recognize that they exist. Then analyze what they are. Finally, mobilize your support just like the captain mobilized air support. For me, my support is God. When I encounter a problem, I pray to God for help.

Zechariah 4:6 tells us, "Not by might, nor by power, but by My Spirit, says the Lord of host."

Psalm 121 reads, "I lift up my eyes to the hills—where does my help come from? My help comes from the Lord, the Maker of heaven and earth."

During our search and clear maneuvers, we didn't have authorization to go into Cambodia. On occasion, we chased the enemy to the border and had to let them go. I'm sure though that we went into Cambodia lots of times unintentionally because the exact location of the border was unclear. We had our designated points where we thought the border was but who knew for sure if that was correct.

Another time, the company flew by helicopter to an area near the Cu Chi Base Camp. We did security patrols outside the base for about four days. Tired, muddy, and hungry, my squad looked rough. I decided to take them into Cu Chi. We walked in through the main gate and looked for a place to shower and eat. A lieutenant came out of a building. He and his uniform were all neat, clean, and sharp.

He looked at us and started yelling, "Stand at attention! Where is your salute! Your appearance is unacceptable! You're a disgrace to the army!"

I got upset. My men and I put our lives on the line patrolling the bush and this squeaky-clean lieutenant proceeded to treat us this way. I gave the lieutenant a good cussing up one side and down the other. This tweaked his pride. He threatened to have me court-martialed and started whining to a nearby captain.

The captain looked at the lieutenant, looked at us, looked back at the lieutenant, shook his head and said, "Lieutenant, you need to find something else to do and leave these men alone." That captain recognized the hard work and sacrifices my squad put up with for the war. His appreciation made me feel good.

On January 27, 1967, I received orders to take two of my soldiers with me to conduct an LRRP. This mission crescendoed into the fateful ambush that occurred on January 29. Due to the severe wound which I received that night, the military doctor passed verdict on me consigning me to the morgue. I have no recollection of traveling from Dau Tieng to Cu Chi, nor of the morgue which would become my temporary abode until my body got tagged and bagged for the trip home to my family.

CHAPTER 5

Resurrection

On January 31, 1967, I woke up in a hospital at Cu Chi. The Seventh Surgical Hospital and the Twelfth Evacuation Hospital operated there at that time.

I asked a nurse, "Where am I?"

She said, "In the hospital. We got you from the morgue. You had lived."

To my surprise and joy, David laid awake in the bed next to mine. Thank God, we were alive! God's mercy brought us through. I was extremely glad to see him. We made it. We were going to live.

I asked him, "What do you remember about the ambush?

He replied, "Well, one of them walked up to my machine gun position at the end of the ambush line and literally stepped on me. I don't remember much else. The fighting, the chaos, the hand-to-hand combat. It's all a blur."

I figured that when David got stepped on, he wheeled around with his machinegun and shot the Vietcong soldier. Then he got shot in the stomach repeatedly by the enemy in response. David and I continued to talk for a bit.

Then, David said, "I'm thirsty." He reached for a bottle of water sitting on a cart between our beds, took a drink, then suddenly slouched motionless, expressionless on his bed.

A nurse checked his vital signs, pulled the sheet up over his head, and said, "He's dead."

I only got to see him for a few minutes. I wondered if he hung on to make sure that I was okay and now he was gone. Anguish devoured my joy instantly. I hated life.

The nurse asked me, "Do you want to talk to the priest?"

I said, "No, I don't want to talk to nobody!"

I didn't understand how he survived the ambush, made it to the hospital, yet they couldn't save him. I also brooded over the guilt that I lived but he didn't. Looking back now, I wished I had gone to see his family in Michigan when I got out of the army. Because of the way events unfolded when I got back to the states, I never did. That haunted me more than anything.

Later that day, the doctor who operated on me told me that I had lost my right kidney and had extensive nerve damage on my right side. Having watched David die, I thought that I was going to die too since one of my kidneys was gone. The doctor explained to me that I could live a healthy life with only one kidney. He told me that if I drank a beer a day that I would be just fine. I didn't know if he was joking but I never did that. The doctor said the nerve damage would be the main concern. I had sharp pain in my right side for years, like a knife jabbing into me. At the hospital there in Vietnam, I had one operation in which they removed a lot of shrapnel from my side, had some blood transfusions, and had to use catheters.

I had a foggy recollection that days later, someone from the battalion visited me. He told me that we had killed a lot of the enemy during the ambush. They counted thirty-five dead Vietcong soldiers at our ambush site. No telling how many more died from the encounter that the enemy dragged off in addition to their wounded. The visitor said that if we hadn't called in the artillery, all of us probably would have died. The artillery created a big ditch like a mote between us and the enemy. This visit cheered me up. The visitor said we did a great job that night and that he was extremely proud of us. I couldn't recall who that visitor was, but I slowly began to feel human again. I accepted the fact that I lived. I concluded that I was just going to go on with life.

After two weeks in the hospital in South Vietnam, I transferred to the 106th General Hospital in Yokohama, Japan.

As I got ready to leave, a nurse asked, "Do you have anything that you want to take with you?"

I replied, "Nothing but the map I had the night of the ambush patrol, the map I bled on."

She said, "We can't let any of the maps go out of the country." Because I insisted, the nurse finally relented. "Okay, I could get court-martialed for this, but I will go get your map."

She hid it in my pajamas. (I still have the map today framed on a wall.) They wheeled me out of the hospital on a gurney and took me to the airfield. Placed on a medical transport plane, I went to Japan. About fifteen to twenty other patients also took that flight, along with attending medical personnel.

I spent six weeks in the hospital at Yokohama, Japan. I went to the mess hall one day. After getting my tray of food, I looked for a place to sit and eat. I turned and saw this guy sitting with his head bandaged up. He sat by himself at a table.

Startled, I said to myself, "It can't be!"

He looked at me with shock on his face. I walked over and sat down. It was Warren from Korea.

The first words out of his mouth sputtered, "Ah, ah, ah, I tell you, Mays, I lost your home address. I meant to send you the money."

He didn't say, "Hi." He didn't say anything salutary or polite. He didn't even say, "Go to h——!"

The first words from his frantic mouth were that he lost my address. If I never got the fifty dollars, the look of fret on his face was worth it. Twelve months and almost twenty-five thousand miles later, I ran into him in a hospital in Japan, both of us injured. It was priceless. That was the last time I saw Warren. The army sent him to a hospital in the states. He asked for my home address again and assured me that he would send the fifty dollars. (I'm still waiting for it today.)

Two months after the ambush, I walked on my own and had no more need of catheters.

One day, a lieutenant came up to me and asked, "What is the closest army base to your hometown?"

I replied, "Fort Campbell, Kentucky, sir. It's about fifty miles from Nashville, Tennessee."

The lieutenant then said, "Okay, we will transfer you there for the rest of your convalescence."

Happy to hear that, I had not been home for about a year. Excited to see my family again, I wrote a letter to Mom telling her that I would be reassigned to Fort Campbell. About two days later, they rolled me out of the hospital in nothing but my pajamas and put me on an air force plane to go home. We flew for about six hours and landed. I assumed we landed in Nashville.

I asked an air force guy, "Excuse me. Where are we?"

He said, "We're in Honolulu, Hawaii at Hickam Air Force Base. This is as far as we go."

They took me off the plane. I sat on the tarmac for a couple of hours with nowhere to go. The sun beat down on me, the air hot and humid but not as bad as Vietnam. I could feel a cool ocean breeze from time to time. Planes landed and took off. Servicemen performing their duty walked by giving me odd looks.

I could almost hear their thoughts, "Why is a guy in pajamas sitting on the hot tarmac?"

I must have seemed a pathetic sight. I had no clothes, no paperwork, and no orders. The only thing I had to my name was my dog tags. Tired, hungry, and depressed that we didn't land in Nashville, I felt completely abandoned.

After some time, an air force guy said to me, "We have to get you to the Schofield Barracks Army Base."

He drove me there by jeep and pulled up in front of a building. Unsure of things, I gave him a blank look.

He said, "Go on. Get out of the jeep and go inside."

As I exited the jeep, he sped off, leaving me standing in my pajamas in front of the headquarters of the Twenty-Fifth Infantry Division.

I cautiously walked into the headquarters surrounded by a cloud of uncertainty. Once inside, everything stopped as I stood in a sea of silence. Déjà vu, peopled stopped what they were doing and looked at me in amusement and curiosity.

The disbelieving expression on their face declared, "What is this guy, showing up here in pajamas?"

After what seemed like an eternity with all eyes of the world upon me, work in the office began to return to normal. The people there turned out to be extremely nice to me. They took me in, gave me a room in the barracks, and finally got me some clothes. My barracks room was ten feet by ten feet with scant furniture. I absolutely loved it! It was the best accommodations I had in a long time.

The army lost my personnel, pay, and medical files, so I never got paid my entire time in Hawaii. No one had computers back then. Everything got resolved by phone calls and using official files for personnel and pay records. Fortunately, the army gave the enlisted soldier three hots and a cot. I also got a standard set of army issue uniforms: class As, fatigues, boots, everything. After a few days, a gruff and gritty first sergeant arranged my assignment to the Hawaiian Armed Services Police (HASP), a joint military police outfit that operated in Honolulu. For the next six months, I worked as a desk sergeant in charge of police patrols.

HASP had its own compound near Waikiki Beach. As the only combat veteran in the unit, I got treated like royalty by the other military members. I never spent a dime on anything while there, which was a good thing because I never got paid either. If the guys went out for pizza, they took me along for free. If they went to the movies, they took me along for free. They really appreciated the sacrifices and hardship I went through in Vietnam.

On weekends, we packed the police station with sailors, marines, soldiers, and airmen destined for the drunk tank. If someone behaved belligerently, we put them in a solitary padded cell to prevent them from getting hurt. One night, a patrolman brought in a drunk petty officer second class, an older guy who had about twenty years of service. He hollered and cussed as I wrote him up. Then we took him to one of the solitary holding cells.

As I opened the cell door, the petty officer suddenly swung and hit me right in the jaw, sending me halfway down the hallway, almost knocked out. He had no reason to jump me. I didn't do anything to provoke him. I just did my job. The patrolman grabbed him and threw him into the cell. About a month later, I had to go to his court-martial hearing. The navy busted him down to seaman. I felt terribly bad for him. The guy had deeply apologized to me.

After a few months in Hawaii, I finally got a bunch of mail that the army forwarded to me from Vietnam. The only family members that wrote to me in Vietnam were my mom, sister, and uncle. I also had a pen pal who wrote to me through an adopt-a-serviceman program. Letters we wrote from the warzone had to be very simple and nondescriptive. We couldn't talk about missions and operations we did. Mom wrote several letters recently to my Vietnam address. Eager to see me again, she asked what was going on, when would I arrive at Fort Campbell. By the time I received these letters, Mom already knew that I was in Hawaii. A few weeks after my arrival here, the Red Cross contacted her by phone and told her my situation.

Now that I was in Hawaii, I had time to consistently write to my pen pal Gloria. Mom submitted my picture, name, and military address to the Nashville Banner for its adopt-a-serviceman program. I had several potential pen pals to choose from. I chose Gloria because she sent a picture of herself in a bikini standing in the snow. She was the cutest little thing! (Don't judge me. I was a twenty-year-old American kid who just came from combat.)

In July of 1967, I got a phone call one day from a man who said, "Sergeant Mays, I want you in full uniform tomorrow at zero seven hundred hours in the morning. A car will pick you up and take you to see Major General Roy Lassetter, Jr., Commanding General of the US Army Hawaii."

I thought maybe I had done something to get court-martialed. I had a sleepless rough night but was ready at seven o'clock as ordered. The car picked me up and took me to the headquarters building located at Schofield Barracks. Inside, a captain sat at a desk and informed me that I was going in to see the general.

He said, "Go into his office, stand at attention, and salute until the general returns your salute."

At this point, I still didn't know why I was there. Only twenty years old and petrified to see the commanding general, I went into the office. Reporters, a TV camera, and other people crowded in there. I still didn't know what was going on. I reported to the general who stood up. Then a captain started to read General Orders Number 673, awarding me the Silver Star for gallantry in action, one of the highest awards given in the army.

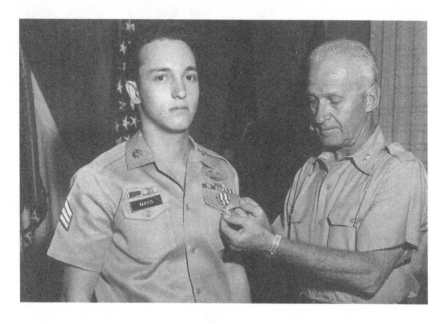

Receiving the Silver Star from Major General Lassetter, Jr.

Sergeant Mays distinguished himself by heroic actions on 29 January 1967, in the Republic of Vietnam. Sergeant Mays was patrol leader of a sixteen-man ambush patrol in the Don Dien Michelin Rubber Plantation, north east of Dau Tieng. The patrol made contact with an estimated thirty-five-man Viet Cong force. The enemy was quickly reinforced, and the patrol was nearly surrounded. Sergeant Mays quickly withdrew his men from their original ambush positions and set up a perimeter. After having his patrol establish their perimeter, Sergeant Mays realized that he was short one man. A check revealed that the man had been wounded and was in the extreme right sector of the ambush. Sergeant Mays directed the forward observer to call in artillery close to their position. With complete disregard for his own safety, Sergeant Mays led several men from the perimeter in an attempt to rescue the wounded man. While trying to get the man back inside the perimeter, Sergeant Mays and three other men were hit by grenade shrapnel. Unable to return to the perimeter, Sergeant Mays directed defensive fire against the Viet Cong who were trying to overrun their position. His unimpeachable valor in close combat against heavily armed enemy forces is in keeping with the highest traditions of the military service and reflects great credit upon himself, his unit, and the United States Army.

Somebody from my unit submitted a recommendation to award me this medal. So, in the general's office, I receive the Silver Star along with the Purple Heart. I felt a great relief that I got awarded and not court-martialed. As the orders were read, I thought of David Berkholz and the ultimate sacrifice that he made. After the ceremony, I felt proud that I had served my country well.

I thoroughly enjoyed my time in Hawaii. Grateful to be alive, I had no bitterness over missing out on promotion to second lieutenant. The army offered me a large reenlistment bonus if I stayed in. However, I had to transfer to a noncombat skill because of my injury. I had what the military called a medical profile, which limited me on the things that I could do. I didn't want to be a desk jockey for the rest of my life, so I decided to get out of the army. If I could have stayed in the infantry, I would have made a career of it. I achieved the rank of sergeant in a little over eighteen months. Along with the medals I received, I thought I could have advanced in rank quickly. But things just didn't work out that way.

In September of 1967, I arrived at the US Army Overseas Replacement Station located at the Oakland Army Base in California. I spent three days at the processing center. As I walked down the boarding ramp from the plane which landed at nearby Travis Air Force Base, I heard protesters (probably unemployed) yelling "baby killer" and "murderer," their comments sullied with profanity. I never saw any war crimes or atrocities committed in Vietnam. In fact, we gave food to the villagers, especially the children. Our medics conducted clinics providing medical treatment. The protesting didn't make sense to me.

The protesters created havoc outside the fence, screaming and throwing things at the military. The personnel who worked at the processing center told us the war was very unpopular, what we should do about it, what we shouldn't do, and not to wear our uniforms once we got discharged. They advised us to wear civilian clothing when we traveled back home. Because of all this, I felt that the whole country was against me, that somehow, I was a criminal. This was not the country that I left three years ago when I went to Korea. It had changed.

In the 1950s and early 1960s, Americans would readily help one another as if our motto was, "Help your neighbor, help yourself." One could hitchhike and catch a ride anywhere. In 1967, it seemed to me that nobody trusted or cared about anyone else anymore. The thought of hitchhiking never seemed safe to me from then on. America had changed that much in three years.

The processing center calculated my back pay which I finally received. Discharged from the army and stunned at what America had become, I traveled to Los Angeles by car and then took a flight back to Nashville. During the trip, I felt extremely self-conscious. Even though I had no uniform on, the average person could tell that I was military. What did their stares mean? What did they think as they glanced my way? Did they feel sorry for me? Did they despise me? One thing I knew for sure. None of them made me feel appreciated or welcomed. Even when I got home, close family members shunned me. I felt like a second-class citizen because I faithfully served my country in war.

CHAPTER 6

Picking Up the Pieces

When I returned home, Daddy and my brothers continued to shun me. I thought that maybe I earned their respect and consideration, having served my country as a combat veteran. At this time in the 1960s though, the nightly news portrayed the Vietnam veterans as baby killers and terrible people. The country had a perception of us as war criminals. But the American public was misled. I believed this influenced the attitude my daddy and brothers had toward me. It took decades for this perception of the Vietnam veteran to change in the eyes of our society. Truth be told, I never saw any Americans commit atrocities against civilians or prisoners when I served in Vietnam.

I blocked out my military service and Vietnam for forty years. I never talked about it with my wife, children, or friends. All they knew was that I served in the army at one time. I never wore any hat or shirt that said anything military on it for all those years. I spent over half my life in emotional exile.

As I began civilian life, I got a job as an estimator, earning fifty dollars a week for a small plumbing company in Nashville, Tennessee. I lived in Bellevue with Aunt Rosetta and Uncle Clifton. During my military service, Uncle Clifton wrote to me on a regular basis. He enjoyed writing. Uncle Clifton worked for the railroad. They lived a decent middle-class life in a modern house. He treated me with love and more regard than my own daddy. I don't remember Daddy ever giving me anything.

During my childhood, Uncle Clifton randomly gave me a dollar and said, "Here, go to the store and get you something." He was more of a dad to me than my real father.

Now that I was home, I arranged to see Gloria, the cute little lady I chose as my pen pal during my enlistment in the army.

When I called her, she said gleefully, "Meet me at my work, the National Life and Accident Insurance Company, in downtown Nashville at twelve o'clock tomorrow. Then we could go to lunch!"

That night I could hardly sleep. The anticipation of finally meeting the girl in the bikini refused to let me sleep. The following day with Gloria's picture in hand, I nervously sat in the lobby of the building where she worked. At twelve o'clock the elevator doors opened, and a sea of beautiful young women poured out. What a sight to behold after three years of overseas duty! I glanced at the picture and anxiously looked around but couldn't identify Gloria.

I then heard this inquisitive voice behind me say, "Herbie? I'm Gloria."

My heart stopped. I had to muster all my strength just to turn around. I gazed upon Gloria for the first time—she was frumpy and as wide as a doorway!

I thought, "My goodness. All that time I spent writing Gloria thinking she was the girl in the bikini standing in the snow. I got snookered!" (Apparently, people faked their appearance even before Facebook!)

Gloria said with a nervous smile, "You want to go eat?"

Trying my best to disguise my shock, I replied, "Okay," nice guy that I was.

At lunch, Gloria owned up to what she did telling me that she sent a picture of her best friend Becky.

She further said, "This weekend is Becky's birthday. Do you have a friend who could be her date? We can double-date to celebrate."

My cousin Larry agreed to do it. We arrived at Becky's house. I finally met in person the girl in the bikini standing in the snow. What a beautiful gal! Fortunately, Larry had eyes for another woman, so this date didn't mean anything to him. The following day, I called

Becky and we became friends. Gloria and Becky had a big falling-out soon after that. Then Becky and I started dating.

I fell in love with Becky the instant I saw her picture, even more so when I met her in person. Becky possessed a far less flattering first impression of me. She thought I looked so skinny and pitiful having just returned from war. I still hadn't gained the weight that I lost from traveling overseas, getting wounded, and having surgery. But she went out with me on dates anyway. She must have felt sorry for me. Her dad fought in World War II and later died when she was sixteen. Both Becky and her mom had a soft spot for the military. They both treated me with kindness.

I felt ecstatic about life. I had survived war, returned to the states, got a job, and met the woman I wanted to marry. A month later at Becky's house, I knelt on one knee while she sat on the couch.

I said, "Becky, I love you. Will you marry me?"

She accepted and then said, "You have to go tell Mama."

I got up, walked into the den, and told her mother, who gave us her blessing.

We set the original date for June 1968. However, at Christmas 1967, we decided to get married the following month.

When we told Becky's mother, she exclaimed, "You're pregnant! Aren't you? You went and got pregnant!"

Now back then my generation approached courtship differently than later generations. Before we got married, Becky and I abstained.

However, her mama insisted all the way up to the wedding, "Yeah, you're pregnant or you wouldn't have moved the date up." (A year after we got married, we had our first baby.)

The wedding took place at the Eastwood Christian Church on a Saturday night attended by my mom, Aunt Rosetta and Uncle Clifton, and Becky's mother, brother, and sister. It was a very nice small wedding.

Following that, we lived in an apartment for six months. Then we bought a house in Hendersonville, Tennessee using a VA loan. I grew up in an old wooden house with no running water, no indoor plumbing, and a few lights. To me, this was the first real house that

I ever lived in. In five years, I went from a poor country boy to an educated man with a wife, child, job, and modern house.

We lived in Hendersonville from 1968 to 1984. We had two children, Walter whom we called Lee, born January 1969, and Lesley, born January 1973. Fortunately, neither pregnancy or delivery had complications. We were proud of Lee, our first-born child, and absolutely adored Lesley, our baby girl. I did my very best to spoil her. (I still do today.)

Though just kids ourselves, we managed parenthood. Becky possessed wonderful motherly instincts. I learned fatherhood by on-the-job-training. We mastered those cloth diapers, so I guess we did okay. When I got out of the military, I wanted a clan of children. After having a boy and a girl, we decided that we had our hands full. We lived our early adult years as a typical family. Lee gravitated to Becky, while Lesley grew up a daddy's girl.

In the early years of our marriage, Becky and I visited Aunt Rosetta and Uncle Clifton a lot. They were like a mother and father to us. Many times, on Sunday, we went out to their house in Bellevue. I can't remember if my daddy ever saw either of my children. Maybe he saw Lee one time. My mom moved to Georgia. Occasionally, she returned to the Nashville area for a visit.

About the first three or four years of marriage, I had problems. I didn't know what caused them. I had trouble sleeping and sometimes bouts of anxiety. Sometimes I got mad for little or no reason and didn't know why. Little things just agitated me. If I heard a car backfire or similar sound, I became startled and agitated for a good while. Things like that threw me into a foul mood but, fortunately, not to a big degree.

Coming home from Vietnam and the military and getting married four months later required a big adjustment. To resolve this, I buried all that turmoil inside and ignored it. Back then, counseling for PTSD didn't exist. I'm grateful that Becky took her marriage vows seriously and stuck it out for better or for worse. We had our fights but nothing devastating.

As time went by, we started coaching youth baseball and football. Lee and Lesley played a lot of sports. Lee played baseball and football. A tomboy in her early years, Lesley played peewee football, the first girl to do so in Hendersonville. She played tackle because at that age, she was bigger than the boys. She dropped out of football when the boys finally got bigger than she. Lesley didn't want to play softball. She wanted to play regular baseball, so she did. Back then, we spent much of our time at the park coaching or attending ball-games. Both children had a great time playing sports as they grew up. About the age of twelve, Lesley outgrew her tomboy tendencies and focused on makeup and clothes.

I coached twelve years of baseball at the nine/ten-year-old level. It started out as Dixie Youth baseball but later switched to Little League baseball. I also coached about ten years of football at the six/seven-year-old level. I had a friend who wanted to join the Civitan Club, which ran the city park and sports leagues. I joined with him. Originally, I didn't intend to coach, but the club announced that they had a baseball team that needed a coach. I gladly and, as it turned out, naively volunteered.

They had so many boys that year in the nine/ten-year-old cat-egory that the league told each team to cut two or three players to form an additional team. Of course, all the teams held on to their good players. Consequently, the newly formed team was like the Bad News Bears. The league scraped up old uniforms for this unexpected extra team, while the others had brand new uniforms.

I complained to the league commissioner, "Look, my ball play-ers don't have nice-looking uniforms like the other teams."

He replied, "Sorry, but your team came into the league late. We already had the uniforms ordered. You will have to wait another two years before we order more."

I made a deal with him, "If this team wins the championship, will you buy them new uniforms next year?"

He scoffed, "Herbie! I have seen those kids! Half of them can't even catch a baseball! If you win the championship, we'll buy them the best uniforms in the league!"

I started eagerly coaching those boys. They were something to behold...but not in a good way. In my heart, I started to agree with the commissioner. Regardless, I taught them the basics of playing baseball and began to encourage them just like Ma Lincoln encouraged me. This scrawny, stuttering farm boy now had an education, modern house, good job, family, and coached sports. Why not inspire these kids to reach for lofty goals?

At every practice, I told them, "All of you are the boys that the other teams didn't want. These other teams don't think you're good enough. But, I know that each one of you is just as good, if not better, than any other player in the league. If you believe in yourselves, then no other team in the league can beat you because you are champions."

By the end of the season, my boys believed and proved it. Positive confession and encouragement became a central part of my coaching style.

We also had a bit of good fortune. As I drove home from work one day on a back road of Hendersonville, I saw a black kid in his yard throwing a baseball with his daddy. I pulled up in the yard and talked with them.

I asked, "Do you play baseball?"

He replied, "No, sir. I don't."

I inquired, "Would you like to?"

He exclaimed, "Yes, sir! I would love to play baseball!"

It turned out that his daddy pitched years ago in a negro league. At this time, his daddy was a fairly old man and had this young boy named Sammy who was nine years old. I told Sammy I would get him on my team.

Sammy, a skinny little kid with thin arms, pitched left-handed, which you didn't see much of in youth baseball. His daddy worked with him so much that Sammy pitched unusually well for his age. Sammy could throw the ball wherever the catcher put the mitt. He was that good. He didn't throw hard, but he could hit the mitt wherever you wanted. I told Sammy that I would come by his house every day and work with him.

I called the commissioner and asked, "I met a nine-year-old boy who would like to play baseball. Can I sign him up for my team?"

The commissioner said, "Yes, sign the boy up and put him on your team." He didn't care.

Every day, I finished working for the post office at two thirty in the afternoon and drove right by Sammy's house on the way home. So, I pulled in. We threw the ball a little bit. I worked with Sammy to maintain his ability to hit the mitt every time no matter where I placed it. Sammy and I did this in addition to regularly scheduled team practices.

Becky and I invited Sammy and his two sisters to our house to play with Lee and Lesley. They were all about the same age. The first time that we had them over, Becky got a phone call from the neighbor who had two boys.

The neighbor lady got extremely upset, demanding, "Who are these little n—— out there in your yard playing with your children?!"

Becky proceeded to have a heated conversation with her on the phone. The neighbor lady refused to let her boys out of the house when Sammy and his sisters visited. Our neighbors didn't like it. This didn't deter us. We had them over frequently. Fortunately, we only suffered verbal harassment, which didn't escalate into vandalism or violence.

We lived in a nice area of town. Sammy and his family didn't. We cared deeply about them. We did Christmas with them and such. As far as my family was concerned, skin color didn't matter. We saw everybody as equal. Growing up with Tom and Mary Hughs ingrained that in me. Becky and I instilled that into our children. Lee and Lesley loved Sammy and his sisters.

About 1974 or 1975, Hendersonville didn't have many black folks living there. The only black boy in the entire baseball league at the time, people gave me grief for bringing Sammy into the league. The first game of the year, we took the field in our scraggly-looking uniforms with Sammy on the mound.

The spectators yelled ungracious comments, "Where did this n—— come from? How did a n—— get into the league?"

Sammy never lost a game. I taught the catcher to take his que from me. I told him where to put the catcher's mitt to set Sammy up for his pitch. Sammy hit the catcher's mitt every time. He struck the batters out and struck them out and struck them out. A few got hits off him. With Sammy, a few other good players, and the rest of the boys believing in themselves, our team went twelve and three that season. We won the championship with the boys that nobody else wanted. Sammy pitched all the way through high school and got a baseball scholarship to a junior college.

I enjoyed coaching youth sports, building up their confidence in themselves and their abilities. I always had good teams. My teams won the championship many times in both baseball and football. Hendersonville had so many kids playing football that the city had its own independent league. Then at the end of the year, the championship team played the champions from another league as the big game of the season finale.

Hendersonville grew tremendously during the 1970s, as many people moved out of Nashville to the suburbs. When I first moved to Hendersonville in 1968, it was still a farming community. We saw the city grow and had the opportunity to positively touch the lives of many kids. Back then, there was no soccer. Kids played either baseball or football.

After two years at the plumbing company, I started working for the post office, a job I held for seventeen years but got credit for twenty due to my military service. Becky and I wanted her to stay at home with the children in their younger years. To afford this, I worked at the post office as well as a part-time job during most of their childhood. I worked nights at Sears in Madison, Tennessee on the warehouse docks five days a week about five hours a night. I went in at seven o'clock to about midnight. Sometimes we worked on Saturdays.

I did this for about seven to eight years starting in 1973. I got off from the post office at two thirty in the afternoon, went home, and got ready for baseball or football practice which would occur about four o'clock. Then I went home for dinner and went to my night job. I got about four hours sleep a night. Being so busy all the time helped suppress my inner turmoil because I just didn't have time to sit around and dwell on the horrors of my combat experience.

Despite my two jobs, we lived paycheck to paycheck. My house note back then demanded $150 a month. I only made $3.25 an hour at the post office and about $2.00 an hour at Sears. Minimum wage at the time yielded $1.60 per hour. Becky stopped working when Lee was born. So, I eventually picked up the part-time job to have enough income. It seemed like we made it okay, but in a manner of just getting by. We didn't buy things for ourselves that much. We shopped mostly for the children. Becky's mother, a truly loving grandmother, helped greatly. Each year, she bought clothes for our children for the new school year.

While working for the post office, I was the substitute courier for the mail route that had the Eleventh Street Assemblies of God Church. I walked that route in East Nashville on Mondays. The routes in East Nashville were park and loop. We drove to the end of the street and then looped the street delivering mail. Then we got back in our vehicle and drove to the next street and did it again. However, I walked to this particular route on Mondays because it sat near the post office. I picked up the mail that I delivered from a relay box.

The Eleventh Street Assemblies of God Church had a mail slot in the main office door. As I walked up on the porch of the church, I heard these women praying loudly using strange words.

I thought to myself, "What in the world is going on?" I lifted the mail slot in the door and just crouched there for a few minutes listening. I peeked in through the mail slot to see what went on. I saw them walking around speaking loudly in a strange language but couldn't make out any faces. After a few minutes, I slid the mail in. This became my routine there every Monday.

The postman who regularly did this route preached for the Church of Christ. I asked him what the deal was at the Eleventh Street Assemblies of God Church.

His eyes wide with concern, he exclaimed, "I'm telling you right now, Herbie, all that speaking in tongues stuff is from the devil!" Pointing his finger at me authoritatively, he declared, "Now you watch yourself when you deliver mail to that church." From then on, he brought me literature to read, trying to convert me to Church of Christ.

At that time, my family and I attended a nondenominational church which claimed to be Spirit-filled. However, we never heard a message in tongues or saw anything Pentecostal or charismatic. The only difference between our church and a traditional one was the contemporary music, which, as young adults, we liked compared to the old hymns. We also liked that it only had about fifty people who attended, a small church.

I always spent a few minutes every Monday at the mail slot of the Eleventh Street Assemblies of God Church, crouched there peeking in, an inquisitive look on my face. Twenty-three years old, I never heard about speaking in tongues. This was my first encounter with it. Something about their praying in tongues intrigued me. I can't explain why. It just did. Hearing tongues didn't spook me. To me, it sounded like someone speaking a foreign language. I spent time in Korea and Vietnam. It reminded me of those Asian languages. Many years later, I finally found out that speaking in tongues was an empowering gift from God.

Becky and I raised our children in church. I knew about God but didn't know God personally. We attended the nondenominational church in Hendersonville for many years. Then we started driving up to White House, Tennessee to attend church with Becky's sister. A Baptist preacher received the baptism in the Holy Spirit with the evidence of speaking in tongues. He started a church in White House called Trinity Fellowship Church. Unusual for this part of the country, Trinity strived to be a true Spirit-filled church. At this church, I first heard a message spoken in tongues along with its interpretation. Becky explained to me what occurred. She read and learned about spiritual things that happened with Christians in the New Testament.

We attended Trinity for many years. I still hadn't accepted Jesus Christ as my personal Savior and Lord. I still didn't know God personally at this point. Ironically, I served in the church as an usher (called deacons in this church). We greeted people as they arrived for worship services, passed the offering plates, and served communion. As the deacons, we performed these main duties. I held this position as a lost sinner, simply a faithful attendee of church, which I had been all my life.

At the age of twelve, I responded to a call for salvation during a revival at the Baptist church in Bellevue. But, I didn't really understand what I had done or what salvation meant. I did it because others did.

Many times, at Trinity, the Holy Spirit convicted me to get saved. Fearing what people would say or think, I never did. People already considered me saved because I served as a deacon in the church. Well known in White House, I owned a successful business there by that time. I cared more about man's judgement of me than God's. I knew without a doubt that God saved me in Vietnam. Oddly, I didn't seek a personal relationship with God. I got along okay in life, so I didn't feel like I needed to cry out to God.

Most of the preaching back then didn't focus on salvation but on spiritual gifts and faith for a prosperous lifestyle. I called it the *name it and claim it* era. People put forth their faith to receive material blessing but did it with the wrong motives to make themselves wealthy not to benefit the kingdom of God. Many preachers at that time, especially on TV, preached a prosperity message to make themselves wealthy from people's donations. We constantly heard phrases like, "You have what you say," and, "Sow a seed to meet your need."

Even at a Pentecostal church that I attended for years, the church seemed to have a crisis every week. It needed money for this and it needed money for that. Having pastored for twenty years, I never harped on money. I gave people the opportunity to give into the kingdom of God. I believed in tithing. Personally, I gave more than the tithe to God. But I didn't want to put people under condemnation about it. Back then, preachers convinced people that they were lost, hell-bound sinners for not tithing.

I didn't have much enthusiasm for church then. I went because I viewed it as a Sunday obligation. Something good people just did. Also, Becky and I wanted our children to grow up attending church. More in tune with spiritual things, Becky diligently ensured that the family went. For my part, I went to church but agonized about getting out in time to watch football.

Healthy all week long, on Sunday morning I had every ailment known to man: headache, backache, hemorrhoids. My flesh offered up any manner of excuses not to go. Sometimes I skipped Sunday morning church. I never attended Sunday or Wednesday evening services. (Sadly, even today a lot of people are that way. The service can't be too long and must end by a certain time. I believe many churchgoers today are complacent and even backslidden.)

CHAPTER 7

Reaching for the Stars

I worked as a postal courier for about twelve years. Then I started working at the distribution center in Nashville on the midnight shift. I worked in the registry department. We handled receipts that came from the post offices of all the Middle Tennessee counties. We processed the money tickets and prepared deposit slips for the bank runs the next morning. We also handled wire transfers and registered mail.

After seventeen years at the post office, I felt the need to do something else in life, an unknown calling that I had to figure out and tend to. This notion gnawed at me deeply one night, as Becky and I drove back from Memphis after visiting Lee.

About two thirty in the morning, while driving up what we called Bethel Hill Road, these words came to me: "Paint and Paper Store, White House, Tennessee."

The idea of a paint store came to me out of thin air. I had never considered such a venture before in my life. I knew nothing about paint, running a store, or owning a business. At the time, White House was just a small country town.

I mentioned the idea to Becky who seemed indifferent. The next day, I told my brother-in-law, Roger, who liked the idea. The two of us along with a friend, Ron, formed a partnership and started the paint store in a little old building in White House around early autumn 1986. Forty years old, I decided to reach for the stars. None of us knew anything about paint. Regardless, the three of us managed to run the shop and learn the painting business while working our other jobs.

Becky and her sister Joy also worked part-time at the paint store. We all learned to mix paint and take care of customers. We sold a lot of wall paper. Six months after starting the paint store, I had twenty years of service with the post office, so I retired from there. I redeemed the money that I had paid into my retirement fund with the post office, a little over seventeen thousand dollars, and used it to further finance the venture.

To generate business, I went out to jobsites and gave out good quality paint brushes to painters along with our business card. I interacted well with the customers and contractors that bought paint from us. Everyone wanted to talk business with me. Ron aggressively collected the payments. He even went to a contractor's home to request remittance if the contractor stalled on paying us. Our different strengths and talents complimented the business.

About six months later, White House started booming with new construction. Business picked up as we worked with every contractor in town. After one year, Roger resigned from the partnership and started his own paint store in Springfield, Tennessee. At that time, Ron and I each took about two hundred dollars a week salary from the business. Ron continued to work as a musician in Nashville.

To supplement my income, I hired a paint crew to do small residential jobs here and there, mostly repaints. I stayed away from commercial contract work because I didn't want to bid for jobs against my customers, the painting contractors who bought paint from us. During this time, I also built houses to generate some income. State law allowed you to build one house a year without having a general contractor's license. I lined up the subcontractors and managed the overall construction of the house. I built about four or five houses while a business owner in White House.

Shortly after starting the business, I went to a training course given by Porter Paints in Louisville, Kentucky. I learned about pressure washing. Back then, painters didn't clean the surfaces that they painted. The conventional method was to apply the new coat of paint over the existing surface without any cleaning or preparation.

I learned that a clean and prepped surface held new paint better and longer. So, I bought a pressure washer for one thousand dollars. I offered free pressure washing along with any paint job that we did. My competitors didn't. This helped our business grow.

The week after I bought the pressure washer while it sat in the original box in the warehouse area of our building, a guy asked me if he could borrow it. A concrete contractor, he had a big concrete sealant job in Nashville. He offered to rent the pressure washer from me for $1,200 a week. I gladly accepted. At the end of that week, the pressure washer, before I ever used it, paid for itself and generated a small profit.

In 1987, I planned on building a house for my family. A young man named Andy who had just come from Louisville, Kentucky approached me and said that he could build the entire house and save me a bunch of money. At first, I told him that no I would manage the project myself. Andy, however, persisted that he could do it and save me a lot of money. Since he was a pastor's son, I decided to give him a chance. He got the framing, roof, and outside panels done. I paid him for the materials as the project went along.

Andy planned on hanging the drywall himself.

I urged him, "Andy, hire a subcontractor to do the drywall since you have little experience in this area."

He insisted, "If I do it, the cost would be a lot less for you."

I relented to his plan. One day, I went out to the house to check on things. I discovered that Andy hung the drywall from the floor up instead of from the ceiling down.

I asked him, "How are you going to deal with the wide crack between the top of the drywall and the ceiling?"

He replied sheepishly, "I'm going to mud that area in."

I scolded, "You can't mud that much of an area and have it look good. You should have gone from the ceiling down and covered the wide crack at the bottom with baseboard molding."

He grudgingly conceded and did the rest of the drywall my way.

Frustrated with his lack of ability and the poor workmanship, I dismissed him from that job. I supervised the completion of the house myself using subcontractors. As we approached the end of the project, a man arrived representing the materials supplier that Andy used.

He informed me, "Mr. Mays, my company supplied twenty-five thousand dollars' worth of building materials for this project but never received payment."

I replied in confusion, "I gave Andy all the money needed to pay for those supplies."

The man firmly retorted, "Regardless, we never got the money. If we don't, we intend to put a lien for twenty-five thousand dollars on this house."

I stood there motionless, silent, encompassed in disbelief. How could this be? Andy, a pastor's son, embezzled the twenty-five thousand dollars! I called Andy to the house.

Upon his arrival, I snarled at him murderously, "I'm going to tell you right now, if you ever come up this driveway again, I'm going to kill you! You decide. If you want to die, then drive up here again!"

His actions outraged me so much that I quit going to church. I couldn't believe that a pastor's son would do this. I didn't darken the door of a church for over three years. Andy's father heard about what happened and to his credit sought me out. Deeply ashamed, he apologized profusely. He even took out a second mortgage on his home to pay the debt. Even with the lien averted, I still refused to have anything to do with church. I felt that if Christians acted like this, then I had no use for them. During this time, Becky continued to go to church, prayed for me, and believed that God would use me.

Becky confessed Psalm 1 over me: "Blessed is the man who walks not in the counsel of the wicked, nor stands in the way of sinners, nor sits in the seat of scoffers, but his delight is in the law of the Lord, and on His law meditates day and night. He is like a tree planted by streams of water that yields its fruit in its season, and its leaf does not wither. In all that he does, he prospers. The wicked are not so but are like chaff that the wind drives away. Therefore the wicked will not stand in the judgment, nor sinners in the congregation of the righteous; for the Lord knows the way of the righteous, but the way of the wicked will perish."

Attending Eastwood Christian Church while growing up, Becky got saved at an early age. She chased after God with a deep spiritual hunger during our marriage. Reading the Bible daily, she knew more of God's word than I because I didn't like to read. She and her friends attended camp meeting hosted by Kenneth Hagin every summer in Tulsa, Oklahoma. She always had a good and positive attitude no matter what life threw at us. Nothing ever got the best of her except for one thing, when people derided me. That always upset her. Even when I dropped out of church, she never lost hope that one day God would use me in a big way. Outside of God, Becky had been my firm foundation in life.

From time to time, Becky asked if I wanted to go to church with her but never pressured me to do so. She laid pamphlets written by Kenneth Hagin throughout the house in the hope that I would read them. She kept confessing, praying, and believing that I would come to God. Becky continually prayed that I would have a Damascus Road experience like Saul did in the book of Acts. She felt that it would take such an experience for God to get my attention. God and Becky had a plan that I didn't know about.

Saul's Damascus road experience occurred in Acts 9:1–9, which read,

> Then Saul, still breathing threats and murder against the disciples of the Lord, went to the high priest and asked letters from him to the synagogues of Damascus, so that if he found any who were of the Way, whether men or women, he might bring them bound to Jerusalem. As he journeyed he came near Damascus, and suddenly a light shone around him from heaven. Then he fell to the ground, and heard a voice saying to him, "Saul, Saul, why are you persecuting Me?" And he said, "Who are You, Lord?" Then the Lord said, "I am Jesus, Whom you are persecuting. It is hard for you to kick against the goads." So he, trembling and astonished, said, "Lord,

what do You want me to do?" Then the Lord said to him, "Arise and go into the city, and you will be told what you must do." And the men who journeyed with him stood speechless, hearing a voice but seeing no one. Then Saul arose from the ground, and when his eyes were opened he saw no one. But they led him by the hand and brought him into Damascus. And he was three days without sight, and neither ate nor drank.

In 1989 after three enterprising years, I wanted to expand the business by selling and installing carpet. However, Ron didn't. He offered to buy my 50 percent ownership in the paint store. I accepted his offer and opened Carpets Plus at the other end of the same building. I called several major carpet manufacturers that I knew of and asked their local representative to come to my new store and assist me in getting set up and teach me the carpet business. Among those that I called were Philadelphia, Lee, Horizon, and Mohawk.

The only one to respond and help me was the representative for Horizon Carpet, Frank Latham. I went to the bank and took out a five-thousand-dollar loan to get set up. Once Frank arrived and taught me the business, I found out that one carpet job could cost that much in materials alone.

Frank taught me how to do job costing and estimating for carpet installation. The first carpet job that I did involved a bonus room and the stairs leading to it. The bonus room was twenty-four feet by twenty-four feet. Carpet came in twelve-foot-wide rolls. When I calculated the amount of carpet needed, I only used the length, figuring twenty-four feet by twelve feet. I mistakenly gave the customer an estimate half of what it should have been. None the wiser, they thought it was a great price and hired me for the job.

The following day, I realized my mistake. I never told the customer about it. I honored my word and did the job for the price I quoted them. When I installed the carpet, I made sure that I displayed a positive and upbeat attitude. Needless to say, I took a big loss on my first carpet job. However, I received numerous referrals from that first customer. Business escalated as a result.

I did whatever I could to close a sale. If the customer couldn't be home until late at night, that's when I went over there to do the estimate and give a quote. I adjusted my time to meet their needs. I also offered discounts if a customer hesitated on accepting my price. Sometimes I offered extras. I did anything that I could think of to close the sale. Once I arrived at a customer's home, I didn't want to leave without making the sale.

After six months, my business kept two crews busy six days a week installing carpet. Suddenly, I started getting calls from Philadelphia Carpet, Lee Carpet, and Mohawk Carpet asking if I would sell their products. I absolutely refused to meet with any of them. Frank with Horizon was the only one who took the time to help me get set up. Consequently, Horizon Carpet was the only brand that I would sell. Horizon classified me at that time as a red star dealer, which gave me priority in receiving material. After one year, I became one of the top five dealerships in sales for Horizon Carpet in Alabama, Tennessee, and Kentucky.

When I relinquished my ownership in the paint store to Ron, I started bidding on commercial jobs. I would bid for a job offering to do the paint and carpet. Contractors liked this because they only had to deal with one subcontractor to install paint and carpet. Most of my bids involved new residential housing and apartment complexes. During this time, I didn't attend church. However, every week I gave Becky a tithe check to take with her to put in the offering. I believe that faithfully supporting God's kingdom with my finances, coupled with Becky's faithful prayers, gave me favor in conducting my businesses.

CHAPTER 8

Conversion

In August 1990, Trinity Christian Fellowship held a Holy Ghost revival with Pastor Paul Baggett as the evangelist. An old-fashioned Pentecostal, hellfire and brimstone preacher, he had a powerful anointing to draw people to salvation. Becky decided to take a pair of my socks and ask Pastor Baggett to anoint them.

This sounded like a silly thing to do, but 1 Corinthians 1:27 said, "Instead, God chose things the world considers foolish to shame those who think they are wise. And He chose things that are power-less to shame those who are powerful." So, she took my socks to the service and Pastor Baggett anointed them. She then went home and put them in my sock drawer.

I got up the next morning, Wednesday, August 22, 1990. None the wiser, I put that pair of socks on. I had a crew painting an apart-ment complex in the Green Hills area of Nashville. I got in my truck and drove to the jobsite. About halfway there, I experienced severe heat around my feet. They felt on fire. Then the heat moved up my legs. Before I knew it, tremendous heat consumed my entire body. I had the air conditioning on high, which still didn't cool me down. A different sensation than the time I caught fire in Vietnam, this felt like an intense internal hot flash. This bizarre and spectacular fiery sensation raged within me yet didn't burn me up.

God used a similar scenario to get the attention of Moses in Exodus 3:1–4,

Now Moses was tending the flock of Jethro his father-in-law, the priest of Midian. And he led the flock to the back of the desert, and came to Horeb, the mountain of God. And the Angel of the Lord appeared to him in a flame of fire from the midst of a bush. So he looked, and behold, the bush was burning with fire, but the bush was not consumed. Then Moses said, "I will now turn aside and see this great sight, why the bush does not burn." So when the Lord saw that he turned aside to look, God called to him from the midst of the bush and said, "Moses, Moses!" And he said, "Here I am."

I knew that the presence of God dwelt in that truck with me. Without a doubt, something a whole lot bigger than me entered the cab, an awesome almost indescribable presence of a superior being, an existence that I couldn't fully explain but couldn't deny. On I drove, awestruck and unable to rationalize the experience away as the product of wild imagination. It was too real, too awesome. This event didn't scare me because I felt an overwhelming peace the entire time.

I got to the jobsite and asked the men if they needed anything from me for that day. Normally, I spent an hour at the jobsite checking things out. But on this particular day I told my foreman that I couldn't get out of the truck and had to get back to the office. I said this because my body still felt like it was on fire. I turned around and came back to our office in White House. By that time, only my feet remained ablaze. I told Becky that I intended to go look at the house that we were building for resale but that I might go with her to the tent revival that night.

Becky didn't hound me to go to the revival. She didn't even invite me to this one. I had known about it and just decided to go because of my earlier experience that day. Without a doubt, I absolutely knew that I had an encounter with God Almighty. I came home around three o'clock in the afternoon and took a shower.

While getting dressed, I inadvertently put those same anointed socks back on that I wore all day. I had never done that before. Normally, I would put on a fresh pair of socks after showering. We left for the tent revival about six thirty in the evening.

Earlier that day, about two thousand miles away, a young lady wept and prayed while walking along a lonely beach on the coast of Panama. Her heart rent in two, Marissa cried out to God for help, her soul dark and dreary like the stormy sky overhead. She had a deep passion to feed the impoverished indigenous Indians that lived in the mountains of Panama. This desire so deep, she sold her possessions to buy them food. She ran out of resources and beseeched the God Who can make a way when there is no way.

As the stormy sky gave way to sunshine, its warm rays beaming down upon Marissa, God answered her in an audible voice, "Marissa, I am raising up a man tonight to come help you."

Back in White House, Tennessee, I sat in an aisle seat with Becky beside me at the revival. Her sister Joy sat on the other side of Becky.

Becky turned to Joy and said, "Look at his feet. He's wearing the socks that I had the preacher anoint last night. He's been wearing them all day."

Pastor Baggett preached that night on "a span of repentance" from Luke 18.

He declared, "Somewhere under your feet tonight, there's a rich young ruler in hell crying out for another chance! It's too late for him, but it's not too late for you!"

He finished his sermon about nine o'clock. I still sensed the strong presence of God around me.

As people sang praises to God, I alone heard an audible voice say, "You have been dead for three and a half years. I'm going to raise you tonight."

I turned around thinking that the guy behind me spoke. However, he was a Baptist pastor who in the past bought paint at our store. I knew the voice didn't belong to him.

The instant I heard that voice, Becky said, "Herbie, would you like to go up front?"

I replied, "Yeah, I want to go up."

I believed that God tailored the message that night for me. I only had a certain amount of time left to repent before eternal judgement befell me. In addition, that amount of time dwindled quickly. I felt powerless to slow it down or add more time to it. I went to the front of the tent to see what would happen.

I used to tell Becky, "I don't believe in this Holy Ghost stuff, people falling out from the power of God." Ignorant about it, I didn't understand or believe. I saw it happen sometimes in churches that we visited. I went to church my entire life but never heard of or saw things like this. I thought it was just people acting silly. I mocked, "It's always the large, homely Pentecostal women who fall out. None of the young pretty ones do. Something's wrong here. Why is it always the big, fat Pentecostal women?"

Whenever I made a snide remark, Becky quipped back, "The Holy Ghost is going to get you one of these days. If you keep on mocking, He's going to get you!" Becky received the baptism in the Holy Spirit some years back.

I stood at the front of the tent along with some other people. Pastor Baggett walked by, not having touched me or anything. Suddenly the power of God just knocked me down to the ground, an immense power I couldn't resist, a tremendous force that violently jolted me to the ground yet didn't hurt me. At that instance, I knew without a doubt that God existed and more importantly that I needed to take Him seriously. Once on the ground, I felt an overwhelming perfect peace as if all things were right in the world.

I don't remember seeing or hearing anything. People told me that my body heaved, convulsed, and shook for about thirty minutes as I lay on the ground. During this time, the other people who attended the revival kept singing praise songs to God. I remember sitting up foggy headed, reaching into my pocket, and pulling out money.

I then said, "Aren't you people going to take up an offering for this man?" Subsequently, I threw the money on the ground.

At that instant, the Lord knocked me back down again. This time, my spirit left my body and hovered above the church service. While suspended in air, I could see stuff happening, an entirely unreal experience to have. As I hovered, I saw a brilliant white light at the far end of a dark tunnel. Although dazzling bright, it didn't hurt my eyes to gaze upon it. The tunnel came forward and engulfed me. I saw two hands up to the forearm with palms facing me protrude out of the light. I remember seeing a distinct mark on the inner wrist of each hand, a scarring. I didn't know what caused them. (At this time in my life, I had always thought that they nailed Jesus to the cross through the palm of His hands.)

Again, I heard the mysterious voice say, "I am giving you a special anointing tonight. An anointing that if people believe then they will be healed. No manner of diseases will withstand this anointing."

The vision ended. Again, I felt myself lying on the ground. Becky and Joy picked me up and helped me to the car. Wobbly, I didn't have control of my faculties.

Roger mocked, "Had a little too much to drink, didn't you, Herbie?"

Joy shot back, "Shut up, Roger! You need some of it too!"

Becky drove me home. Incapacitated for twenty-four hours in the Spirit, I couldn't function. Although awake, I couldn't do anything. I felt like God poured stuff all over me. During the events of August 22, 1990, I received the baptism in the Holy Spirit with the evidence of speaking in tongues. An incredible conversion experience, I considered it the day that I truly got saved. I stayed home all day on August 23, unable to do anything.

That night, I went to the revival again. As we drove home, I came to a complete stop in the middle of the road.

Becky asked, "What's wrong?"

I told her, "The Lord wants us to go into the mission field. We're to go to Panama and preach the Gospel."

The very place that I swore I would never go back to after completing jungle warfare school.

I had declared, "I will never come back to this godforsaken place again!"

As it turned out, God had not forsaken Panama and commissioned us to help build His kingdom there. At that moment, I surrendered everything to God.

Becky said, "Well, if that's what God wants, let's go then!"

We never fretted over the prospect of selling the house or getting rid of our possessions. We started planning the next day to go into the mission field. At this time, I hadn't told Becky or anyone else about my vision and wouldn't for years. I couldn't figure out why God would choose someone like me to go into ministry. Later, I found out that God often chose the most unlikely people to do things.

God told us, "I want you to go and minister to the Indians of Panama."

Between 1990 and 1993, I made several mission trips to Panama while still running my carpet and paint business. Becky accompanied me on some of them. The name of our ministry was Damascus Road Ministries. We reached out to the Guaymi Indians, making mission trips to Panama every couple of months.

A few days after my conversion, Becky bought me a Bible and wrote in it, "August 22, 1990. To my brand-new (big, fat Pentecostal) husband, I love you with all my heart. Every tear was worth tonight. Every stripe Jesus took was meant for this night. Love, Becky." She inserted *big, fat Pentecostal* because of the snide comments I made in the past about only the big, fat Pentecostal women fell out under the power of God.

As a result of my conversion, all bitterness left me. A calmer person now, I didn't get agitated so easily. I sought out Andy who stole the twenty-five thousand dollars from me. I drove to his work and waited in the parking lot for him. He arrived with a look of grave concern when he saw me there.

I said, "Andy, I forgive you for what you did to me. I choose to love you in the Lord. I have no hard feelings about what happened." Then I left. I never saw him again because he left town shortly thereafter.

The contractor for whom I painted the apartment complex in Green Hills reneged on paying me for the last part of that job. I had painted a lot of houses for him in Spring Hill, Tennessee south of Nashville when that area had a housing boom. Now, I painted a forty-eight-unit condo complex in Green Hills for him. We completed two units a week. I submitted my draw to him on Thursday to get paid on Friday. About halfway through the project, his payments started to get sporadic. He offered up one excuse after another for this. At the end of the job, he owed me for six units, over fourteen thousand dollars in labor and materials.

Other subcontractors grumbled that the general contractor didn't have any money and subsequently started pulling off the job. I had my lawyer check into it and found out that he had a slew of people suing him and that I probably would never see my money. So, I just let it go. Fortunately, I had enough capital in my business that I could cover that loss even though it was tight for a while. I always paid my employees and my bills even if it meant that I wouldn't have any take home money that period. I just put it in God's hand.

After the revival, I became good friends with Pastor Baggett. Six months later, we started attending the Millersville Assemblies of God Church where Pastor Baggett served as the senior pastor. I had decided that I wanted the same anointing on my ministry that he had on his. Over the next few years, I traveled a lot with Pastor Baggett, assisting him with the revivals that he did. I accompanied him on at least one revival a month. He did revivals frequently in the Middle and West Tennessee areas.

Pastor Baggett enjoyed telling the story of what happened to me the night at the revival when I got saved. I believed it pleased him to know that God raised up another ministry out of his. During this time, Pastor Baggett taught me a lot about ministering the Gospel and church operations. He even came with me on a few mission trips to Panama.

In December 1990, when we still attended Trinity Christian Fellowship, Pastor Roy planned a Christmas outreach mission trip to a little Baptist church in Boquete, Panama that he supported. Shortly before the trip, Pastor Roy got injured and couldn't go. His wife, Anne, suggested that I go in his place. The pastor of this little Baptist church was Pastor Rojas. Originally from Chile, he pastored this small church in Panama. Speaking English well, he came to the US many times to raise money for the little church. We arrived in Panama City, Panama on December 4, rented a van, and met up with Victor and Carmen Rojas while at the airport. Victor was Pastor Rojas's son, Carmen his daughter-in-law. We checked into a hotel for the night, while Victor and Carmen stayed with some friends.

The following day, Victor and Carmen returned to the hotel fraught with concern. They frantically informed us that we might not get out of Panama City. Come to find out, the night before, Colonel Herrera, a Noriega supporter, broke out of prison and took over a police station. In fear of a possible coup, Panamanian and US authorities locked down Panama City.

We decided to try anyway. As we got to the outskirts of the city, we encountered a roadblock manned by the Panamanian military which didn't let anyone through. We turned around to go another way. We ran into another military road block that wouldn't let us through either. We tried several routes with the same result. In some instances, the Panamanian military aggressively pointed their assault weapons at us. The entire city was shut down. No one could get out.

Frustrated, Victor said, "There is one more possible road leading out of the city."

Becky suggested, "We need to start praying in tongues for the Holy Spirit to get us out of here."

So, Anne, Becky, another lady that was with us, and I began to pray. Victor and Carmen gazed at us in deep curiosity.

As we drove over the Bridge of the Americas, we passed a hill that had a big sign on it that read, "Jesus Cristo, el Senior de Panama." In English it meant, "Jesus Christ, the Lord of Panama."

We approached another checkpoint, this one manned by the US military. We told them that we were Americans heading out on a mission trip. After looking in our van, they let us through. Relieved and joyous, we proceeded with our eight-hour drive to Boquete.

While in Boquete, Pastor Rojas asked me to preach at the evening service. I agreed even though I never preached before. A nervous wreck that afternoon, I tried to figure out what to preach on.

The Holy Spirit prompted me to preach on 2 Timothy 1:7: "For God has not given us a spirit of fear, but of power, love, and of a sound mind."

The service started at six o'clock that night. The church building was made of concrete blocks with a metal roof. Between the top of the walls and the roof were gaps so that air could circulate since the building didn't have air conditioning. All manner of birds flew in and out of the church randomly. The congregation sat on folding chairs.

As the service started, the congregation sang a few songs. When I got up to preach, three white doves flew into the church and sat on the large cross hanging on the front wall of the sanctuary. They watched over the service the entire time I preached. Because this little church had no children's church or youth service, everyone attended the main service. During which, no one in the entire congregation uttered a single word while I preached, not a teenager, not a child, not even a baby cry. All the people listened reverently as the translator interpreted the message that night, highly unusual for a gathering that had babies, children, and teenagers.

At the end, I gave an altar call in which several people came up for prayer. One lady named Lupe Sanchez wanted salvation. When I prayed for her, she fell out under the power of God. No one had ever fallen under the power of God before when I prayed for them. Why should they since I was nobody special? This occurred in a Baptist church no less. These people never saw that before. A few others fell as well after I prayed with them. When the service ended, I turned around and noticed that the three white doves had left.

A man approached me and said, "My name is Enrique Sanchez. I would like you and Pastor Rojas to come to dinner at my house tomorrow. I want to know what you did to my wife."

Enrique spoke very good English and got educated in the US. He didn't believe in the baptism in the Holy Spirit. As a Baptist, he believed that when he got saved, he received all the Holy Spirit that he would ever get. I lacked the scriptural knowledge to explain to him that with this baptism, the Holy Spirit gave additional power and gifts to build the kingdom of God. Regardless of this difference in belief, Enrique and I became good friends.

During this trip, I learned that Victor and Carman wanted to build a house in which to live. I decided to help them. In so doing, God showed how He can make all things new again. Over three years ago, a pastor's son swindled me out of twenty-five thousand dollars in the building of my own house. Now, God made it my heart's desire to help this pastor's son build a house for his family. In early 1991, I raised five thousand dollars for this effort and returned to Panama in April and helped them build their house. I spent a month in Panama on this trip.

I told Enrique that I wanted to minister to the Indians in Panama. He introduced me to a man named Moses Vega who lived in David, a city nestled in the mountains which had a large Indian population living in the surrounding jungle. Married with children, Moses was about forty-five years old. He worked oversees as an engineer in the energy industry and earned enough money to retire and become a full-time missionary.

Answering God's call to return to Panama and share the Gospel with the Indians, Moses gave up his lucrative job. His wife, Talsi, did as much evangelistic work as he did. I went with Moses to seek out Indian families with whom to share the Gospel message. They lived in family huts spread throughout the jungle. They didn't live in a clustered community to make up a village. Each family had its own hut and foraged off the land for food daily.

Moses wanted me to meet a missionary couple who lived in San Felix and ministered to the Indians. San Felix sat about fifty miles east of David. As I entered their house, Moses introduced me to Marissa and her husband. This couple didn't have a lot of possessions. A lone bed occupied their bedroom. A spare room had two cots in it. A small table sat in the kitchen. Marissa only had two dresses left in her wardrobe. Come to find out, they sold most of their possessions to buy food to feed the Indians living in the mountains.

Such missionaries had to fend for themselves in raising money for their efforts. Since the Indians lived in poverty, they had no money to contribute. The only economic opportunity that the Indians had was during harvest season on the plantations. Other than that, they lived off the jungle. Marissa and her husband received a scant monthly stipend from a supporting denomination, but the rest was up to them.

Dedication ceremony for the feeding center in San Felix, Panama.

Marissa spoke English well, but her husband didn't. We conversed for a while, as I expressed that I came to share the Gospel and help the Indians any way that I could.

With a glow on her face and hope in her voice, Marissa asked, "May I show you gentlemen something?" She escorted us to the kitchen which had a calendar hanging on the wall with the date of August 22, 1990 circled. She asked me, "Does this date mean anything to you?"

I replied, "Yes, it does. I got saved on August 22, 1990."

Marissa immediately started praising God. She then told us about the events she experienced that day on the beach as she prayed to God for help to feed the Indians. She reached toward me and asked, "May I touch you? You must be an angel from God."

Observing all this in awe, tears began to stream down Moses's face. At that moment, I decided to help Marissa build a feeding center.

I returned to Tennessee and began raising money for this endeavor. About three months later, we raised five thousand dollars in donations from a handful of people who attended the Millersville Assemblies of God Church. After collecting enough money, Becky and I returned to San Felix in the fall of 1991 along with several people from church. We bought materials to build a center that had storage, a shelter with a cooking pit, and feeding area. Local stores donated food items. Also, Moses had several contacts from which fruits and vegetables were donated.

We dedicated the feeding center and conducted a medical clinic, too. We also gave the Indians hygiene items like toothpaste. One of the local couples volunteered to cook food at the center daily to give the Indian children one good meal a day. Once word got out, scores of children came out of the surrounding jungle daily to eat at the center. We fed them rice, beans, fruits, and vegetables. Occasionally the feeding center had beef or chicken to cook.

On the plane trip back to the US, Becky confided that she really didn't want to go back to Panama. She grew up as a city girl not used to the jungle or mountains. She experienced culture shock. Abiding in small towns in the mountains and jungles of a third world country didn't appeal to her. As for me, I grew up in the country, trained in Panama during the military, and lived in the jungles of Vietnam. I adjusted to this environment easily. However, within two days, God melted Becky's heart as she constantly thought of and talked about the little children living in poverty and how precious they were. At that point, she decided to give up all creature comforts for the sake of the ministry.

Over the next few years, I traveled several times to Panama. Sometimes Becky went with me. I usually stayed about two weeks. During this period, Moses and I sought out Indian families in the mountains. I also preached in churches here and there with the help of an interpreter.

My first time driving in Panama, our interpreter, Arturo, met us at the airport. We rented an SUV and headed to Boquete along the Pan-American Highway with Arturo in the passenger seat and Becky in the back. On the way, I passed a car while crossing over a bridge. No sooner had Arturo informed me that passing on a bridge was illegal in Panama, flashing lights and a siren seized our attention, as a young policeman pulled us over.

Parked on the side of the road, I took out my Tennessee driver license and handed it to the police officer. He looked it over while scolding me in Spanish. His speech steadily escalated into a harsh rebuke. I mean, he proceeded to read me the riot act. While the policeman ranted for well over five minutes, I sat there with a silly grin on my face, nodding my head periodically. I felt like Lucy when scolded by Ricky Ricardo in Spanish.

Having no idea what the policeman said, I occasionally replied, "Si. Si, senior. Si."

Because the officer seemed highly upset, Arturo just sat silently in the passenger seat while uneasiness smothered his countenance. Finally, the police officer asked Arturo if I understood Spanish.

Arturo meekly replied in Spanish, "No, sir. Not a single word."

The young officer, shaking his fist, erupted into profanity and demanded in Spanish, "You mean to tell me that he did not understand a single word that I said this whole time?"

Arturo replied apprehensively, "No, sir. He didn't."

Exasperated, the policeman handed me my driver license and stomped off, waving at us to get going before he changed his mind. By the grace of God, I didn't get a ticket.

During the times when Moses and I shared the Gospel message to the Panamanian Indians who lived in the mountain jungles, we went out for two or three days at a time witnessing to them. Moses built a church in the mountains, and we invited them to go. We tracked through the jungle until we found a hut. Then we shared the Gospel with the Indian family that lived there, asked them if they wanted to get saved, and invited them to attend the church. We also prayed for the sick and handed out aspirin. Moses taught the Bible to the Indians at the church. He wanted to train one of them to take over as pastor.

When witnessing to the Indians, just about every one of them accepted salvation. We didn't have to try to convince them because they were very receptive to the notion of going to heaven. Now whether they actually understood what they did was a different story.

The Indians of Panama were very poor and uneducated and never heard the Gospel message. Therefore, Moses offered to lead them in accepting salvation and then tried to mentor them about stuff in the Bible afterward so that they had a better idea of the Christian faith. Because they didn't have anything, they willingly accepted new things into their lives. We tried diligently to disciple them after they accepted Jesus to make sure that they knew what they did.

The Indians were grateful people. When we shared the Gospel with them, they in turn always wanted to give us something. A simple visit to their home resulted in a gift from them. Generosity and thoughtfulness encompassed their nature. Often the gift was a simple flower, but they always wanted to give something.

On one visit, Moses told me, "This Indian family has invited us to stay and eat dinner with them."

She cooked rice which I liked very much.

I replied, "Wonderful, I'd love to."

To Moses's amusement, I found out that the rice came with chicken feet. He already knew this. They rotated the chicken foot in their mouth while grinding it with their teeth. Then they spit out the toenails.

I toiled in thought, "There is no way I can eat chicken feet!"

While the grown-ups sat in the hut eating dinner, the kids played outside. I received a big plate of rice with two chicken feet. Born and raised in Panama, Moses could eat the chicken feet. Not me! Fortunately, I heard the children playing on the other side of the hut wall where I sat. While pretending to eat the chicken feet, I nonchalantly passed them out through the gap between the ground and the bottom of the wall behind me. Thankfully, the children snatched them up quickly. To complete the charade, I acted like I relished this delicacy. Our hosts asked if I wanted more. I promptly declined and acted full.

During my tenure with Moses, we witnessed to about a hundred Indians one-on-one in the jungle. Just about all accepted the Lord. We did our best to teach them Christianity afterward to ensure that they, in fact, knew that they accepted Jesus as Lord and Savior. Even though uneducated, they were inquisitive and wanted to obtain knowledge. They didn't act like hardheaded know-it-alls that we dealt with here in the US. Moses and I kept the teaching very simple. We taught the basic salvation message. We didn't get into deep theology or detailed instruction of things like the baptism in the Holy Spirit which gave extra ability to do God's work here on earth. We kept it simple with stuff like "God so loved the world," John 3:16. We focused on what would get them to heaven.

CHAPTER 9

Rhema: The Spoken Word of God

In 1993, I told Becky, "I believe God wants us to go into the mission field full time."

Becky suggested, "Perhaps we should go to Bible school first. You're so wild, maybe we need to refine you a bit and increase your knowledge of the word of God."

Becky knew a lot of the Bible because she liked to read. I didn't on both accounts. Even though I went to church most of my life, I didn't know much about the Bible. What I did know, I learned from Pastor Baggett and by listening to R. W. Schambach tapes.

I replied, "I'll pray and fast until God gives me an answer about Bible school."

About the fourth day of fasting and praying, God told me in His silent voice, "I want you to go to Rhema."

I truly felt in my spirit that was what God wanted us to do. We rented out our furnished house in Cross Plains, Tennessee and went to Bible school for two years at Rhema Bible Training College in Broken Arrow, Oklahoma, a suburb of Tulsa where I had traveled during my solo teenage trips. We sold the carpet and paint business to a young man for fifteen thousand dollars. We agreed that he would pay us in monthly installments. This was to help sustain us financially while at college. To our dismay, he only sent one payment. Within two years he went bankrupt. I didn't make a big issue of it. I decided to forgive and look to God for our provision.

We started in September 1993. During our two years at Bible school, neither one of us missed a day of class and were never tardy. We planned to become full-time missionaries after graduation. As the first semester started, I was excited to be at Bible school. A high school drop-out, I wanted to prove that I could get a college degree. I made up my mind that I would not just get by. I wanted to excel in my studies and assignments.

We had some savings built up from the carpet and paint business and didn't owe any money. The only person who supported us financially on a regular basis was a precious black lady who lived in Springfield, Tennessee. We didn't even know her very well either. I had preached at a black church prior to going to Bible school, and we met this sweet lady.

She invited us over for dinner a few times and said, "Let me know when you go to Bible school."

She faithfully sent us a twenty-dollar money order every month, while we studied at Rhema. Each time, we sent her a thank-you note for her generosity. The December of our second year, we received a two-hundred-dollar money order. I didn't know if she really sent that much or if the Post Office printed up a twenty-dollar money order wrong. But we got two-hundred-dollar that year right before Christmas. The last month of school, the money orders stopped.

In addition to this, Becky and I worked as we attended college. During the first six months, we both worked evenings as customer service representatives for a Sears call center. My job was to sell maintenance agreements. When someone bought an appliance, Sears offered them a maintenance agreement as well. All the customers who refused at the time of purchase came up on a print-out thirty days later. My task was to contact those customers by phone and convince them to get the maintenance agreement, a tough endeavor after they declined the first time.

I encountered a multitude of complaints while trying to sell these agreements. People complained about the service they experienced, they didn't get this, or they didn't get that. After a while, I got so tired of the complaints that one night I started giving out the office phone number of the department manager because, as telemarketers, we had no ability to resolve complaints. A week later, our department manager called everybody into a meeting at work.

Mad as a wet hen, she exclaimed, "I'm going to fire whoever gave out my office phone number to complaining customers! If I can find out who you are, you're fired!"

Right then and there, I astutely determined that I ought not give out her office phone number anymore. Fortunately, she never identified me as the culprit.

My last month working at the call center, I sold over thirty thousand dollars' worth of maintenance agreements, making me the top salesman for that month. Each month the call center held a meeting to recognize high performers. For my achievements, management awarded me a can of tuna and a can of tomato soup. (Woohoo!) When I got home, I told Becky that I made salesman of the month.

Thrilled at the news, she inquired, "What did they give you!?"

I proclaimed, "A can of tuna and a can of soup!" Then I concluded that we needed to find better jobs.

The second semester, we cleaned fancy houses because it paid more. During that period, Becky started feeling poorly all the time. One of our main customers was Mr. and Mrs. Chin. Mr. Chin was a psychiatrist.

One day, Mrs. Chin asked me, "Herbie, do you know anyone who can paint houses?"

I said, "Yes, I can paint your house for you."

Her house was a large two-story mini mansion. She asked how much I wanted to paint the eves and downspouts if she bought the paint. An accurate estimate would have been three thousand dollars. Because I needed money, I told her that I would do it for nine hundred dollars. She gladly agreed. It took me about a month to paint the house in my spare time.

I had only one pipe left to paint. Becky and I got home from school and ate lunch.

Then I said, "Becky, I got to go finish painting Mrs. Chin's house."

As I walked out to the truck, the Holy Spirit told me in His silent voice, "Go back in. You and Becky agree that Mrs. Chin will give you $1,450 for painting their house." The Holy Spirit didn't tell me to ask for $1,500, nor $1,400, but for $1,450, an unusual amount.

I thought, "Oh, goodness. This is going to sound crazy. Becky's going to think I'm nuts!" I ignored God, got into the truck, and tried to leave.

God prodded me firmly, "Go back in and get her to agree with you. Go get Becky to agree with you."

I sat there for five minutes as this just swirled inside me. I finally surrendered and went back into the apartment. I stated sheepishly, "Becky, the Holy Spirit told me to have you agree with me that Mrs. Chin will pay us $1,450 instead of $900."

Becky eagerly replied, "Oh yeah, yeah, let's agree!"

Relieved by her response, I agreed with her in prayer and then headed off to Mrs. Chin's house.

When I pulled in, Mrs. Chin informed me, "Herbie, I have to leave but I put your money in an envelope under the flower pot on the table on the back patio. Thank you for the wonderful job."

I painted that last pipe and finally finished the job. I got the envelope and put it in my pocket. As I drove down the road, curiosity got the best of me and I had to pull over and count the money. It was $1,450, exactly what the Lord had told us to pray for.

During our first year at Rhema, I had an assignment to prepare a sermon and preach it in front of the class. They called this lab. They gave us twelve minutes to preach to the class. I had to type up a sermon with a certain number of points, an introduction and a conclusion. It had to have scriptural references. The title of my sermon was "What in Hell Do You Want?"

I gave the instructor, Mr. Cooper Beatty, my assignment sheet and stood at the lectern. The timer bell rang. I took my Bible and slammed it down on the lectern.

I loudly declared, "If you ain't saved, then you're going to hell!"

With eyes wider than a hungry barn owl at midnight, a lady sitting in the front row nearly jumped out of her seat yelling, "Ah!" Embarrassed, she gazed around at the other students who laughed at her reaction.

Becky, attending her class next door, heard all the commotion. Instinctively, she knew that somehow it involved me.

The point of my sermon, hell offers nothing that you want, so don't end up there. I completed my presentation. Then four students picked randomly by Mr. Beatty filled out a critique sheet on my performance. One critique chastised me harshly for irreverent behavior, disrespect toward God, and having a worn-out Bible that looked tattered rather than pristine. She concluded her critique by demanding that I never be allowed to preach anywhere ever again. The other three students gave me a positive critique. When Mr. Beatty gave me his feedback, he noted that what I actually preached did not line up with the lesson plan that I turned in.

I shrugged my shoulders and sheepishly said, "I just say what the Holy Spirit prompts me to at the time."

He smiled and concluded, "Herbie, you will never be able to preach from a prepared sermon. That's just not you. But, just keep doing what you're doing. Everything will be okay. You will be just fine working in the mission field." He gave me an A+ for that assignment.

Shortly thereafter, I prayed alone one evening in our little apartment, while Becky went to work. I had a vision where I saw Heaven. It had seven levels. Which level you could gain access to depended on how you lived your life for God. Everyone who got saved went to Heaven. But in this vision, those who got saved and did nothing for God could only be in level one. The more you did for God in your life, the higher the level you could go, each level more splendid than the previous.

I had never seen that in the Bible. Of course, God hadn't revealed all things to man in the Bible. I did know that Heaven existed, but other than that, the Bible shared very little of what it's like. The vision seemed so real. I spoke to Mr. Beatty about it.

He said, "I have been in ministry all my life and I'm in my seventies. I have never heard that before. But, based on what you have just said, I believe that God genuinely showed you something. I personally wouldn't discredit that at all."

One night in the Spring of 1994, I again spent time alone with God in our apartment, worshiping, praying, and complaining, mostly complaining because Becky and I struggled to make ends meet.

I felt God tell me, "I'm releasing you to tell people about the vision you had when I placed the healing anointing on you."

Later that week, Pastor Baggett called me from Tennessee and invited me to preach that Sunday evening at the Millersville Assemblies of God Church. I was broke. It was a twelve-hour drive to Millersville from Broken Arrow. If I preached, then I would have to drive all through the night to be in class Monday morning. I accepted the invitation.

At that Sunday evening service, I shared for the first time the vision that I had during my conversion. The Holy Spirit saturated that sanctuary with His presence. People fell out under the power of God all over the place.

After the service ended, a lady came up and told Becky, "It's unbelievable! Herb's anointing is as strong as Pastor Baggett's!"

I believe this occurred because I had spent so much time with Pastor Baggett. It was like the relationship that the prophet Elijah had with his protégé, Elisha. Pastor Baggett took up an offering and presented us with a check for eight hundred dollars. I wholeheartedly believed that God told Pastor Baggett to invite us because we desperately needed the money.

We came back to Tennessee during summer break between the first and second year of school. A friend of ours whom we went to church with, Dot Patrick, let us stay for free in a cabin that she had on her property in Cottontown. I painted houses to raise money for the next school year. Becky went to a medical appointment and found out that she needed a hysterectomy. We didn't have medical insurance or the money for that kind of surgery. We put our trust in God to take care of the situation.

Consequently, Becky didn't work that second year of school so she could rest up and concentrate on her studies. We lived almost daily on tuna and macaroni and cheese because it cost less than a dollar for us to eat a meal. We no longer indulged in luxuries or extras like we did when we owned a successful business. Becky couldn't get her hair or nails done whenever she wanted like before, no more vacationing in Hawaii. This experience stretched our faith. The hard times we went through gave us a greater appreciation for things.

As the second year of Bible college started, I worked as a maintenance man for the First Baptist Church of Broken Arrow, an extremely large church. They had over five thousand members. Even though most Rhema students spoke in tongues, this church liked to hire Rhema students because we proved to be excellent employees. Out of courtesy, we never spoke in tongues or talked about anything that contradicted the Baptist faith while we worked at the church. In return, the church treated us well. They were a good employer.

I opened the buildings on Sunday morning, changed light bulbs, cleaned, things like that. I made $5.50 an hour. As a large church, it had its own business manager to run the day-to-day operation. What I liked best about the job was that the Baptist always had food with every event. When we went through the buildings cleaning up after an event, we had our fill of the leftover food, especially donuts on Sunday morning!

One Sunday morning during the winter of 1995, snow and ice blanketed the Tulsa area, the air bitter cold. I had the task of putting salt out on all the sidewalks and scraping up the ice before people arrived for service. As I walked through the back door into the gymnasium to cut the heat on, discontent got the better of me as I complained to God. I shivered in the cold, my only footwear a pair of tennis shoes with slits worn in the sides, hardly appropriate for this weather. Wet and numb, my feet ached. I used to be a successful business owner but now at the age of forty-eight only made $5.50 an hour. It was all we could do to earn enough money to pay for tuition, rent, utilities, and food. By this time, we often got food from the food bank at the Baptist church. Disillusioned and upset, I turned my anger toward God.

While walking through the gym, I heard an audible voice say, "Because you are faithful, I am going to do more in ten years with your ministry than most people do in a lifetime who graduate from Rhema."

Stunned, to say the least, I looked around...not a soul in the gym to behold. While I stood there, the weight of my burdens, self-pity, and discontent suddenly evaporated. Joy unspeakable flooded my being. I went outside and shoveled salt, snow and ice singing loudly while ignoring my frozen feet. For the rest of my time at Rhema, I had a good attitude because I took my eyes off the unpleasant circumstances that I experienced and focused on God.

One Friday afternoon during our last semester, Becky and I got finished with our classes at noon. As we walked through the door of our apartment, the phone rang. On the other end, Pastor Baggett invited me to preach the evening service that Sunday in Millersville. We agreed. Becky and I packed up and headed out getting to Nashville early Saturday morning. I preached the following night. At the end of the service, Pastor Baggett gave me a check that I folded up and put in my coat pocket. I never looked at the check and threw the coat in the back seat of my car.

We headed out and drove all night to return to Broken Arrow for class the next morning. When we got to our apartment, I finally looked at the check, which was for $1,500! We never discussed our financial situation with Pastor Baggett ever. However, this was the second time he financially blessed us when we really needed it while attending Bible school.

Two weeks before I graduated from Rhema, the business manager of the Baptist church called me into his office and said, "Herb, I know that you graduate in a few weeks and want to go to the mission field. However, would you consider working here permanently? I talked it over with the deacons. We want to offer you a full-time job here. You are one of the best employees we have ever had. We will start you out at eleven dollars an hour, give you three weeks of paid vacation, and pay all your insurance."

Taken aback, I replied that I would think about it. I went home and discussed it with Becky. This offer doubled my pay, I liked my job there, and we would have benefits to pay for Becky's operation.

Becky responded, "Well, what did God tell you to do?"

That ended the discussion right there. God didn't tell me to be a maintenance man. He called me into the mission field. I had looked at the situation through natural eyes, thrilled at the prospect of making more money and getting Becky her operation.

I returned to the business manager's office and said, "I greatly appreciate the offer. But, I can't accept. I'm going to the mission field."

The business manager replied with a smile, "I knew that was going to be your answer."

In June 1995, I graduated with a 3.92 GPA and a ministerial degree focusing on missions. Becky graduated with a 3.94 GPA and a degree concentrating on what they called the ministry of helps. Pastor Baggett and his wife, Abby, drove up to Broken Arrow to attend our graduation ceremony at Rhema. Pastor Baggett invited me to be a member of his pastoral staff at the Millersville Assemblies of God Church. Deeply honored, I had to decline his offer because God called me into the mission field.

As with the usual flow of life, this was a bittersweet moment. After sacrificing, working hard, and struggling for two years, we were now ordained ministers. However, Becky and I returned to Tennessee broke, unemployed, and with no medical insurance.

CHAPTER 10

Into All the World

We again attended the Millersville Assemblies of God Church. Becky still needed the hysterectomy operation. I started painting houses again to generate money to pay for her operation and to fund our mission ministry to Panama. Brother Baggett, good friends with the president of Baptist Hospital, once again blessed us tremendously.

One day we receive a phone call at home from a nurse who said, "We would like to set up an appointment for Becky to see a doctor. The president of Baptist Hospital called us and requested that you receive a thorough examination and operation. Baptist Hospital will pay all the cost."

We joyfully accepted the offer! When we arrived at the appointment, we found out that the doctor was rated as the number 1 gynecologist in Nashville. After examining Becky, he concluded that she needed a full hysterectomy, which would resolve her current medical issues. He set her up for an operation the following week.

I told the doctor, "I don't have any money or medical insurance. I have no way of paying you for any of this."

The doctor replied, "You don't owe me anything. We are doing everything free. It won't cost you one dime. I go to First Baptist Church Capitol Hill in Nashville. I provide medical treatment to all their staff free of charge. If they send me patients, I do it for nothing. God has blessed me, so I am going to bless you just like I bless the staff at my church."

We gladly accepted their kindness. The doctor's office called Baptist Hospital and set up the operation. That morning, we walked into the admissions office and Becky stated her name.

The lady working there said, "Okay, come along with me." She escorted Becky to the pre-operation preparation area.

We didn't sign anything. We didn't fill out any paperwork. We didn't do anything. The admissions lady introduced me to a nurse who ran the floor where Becky would recover.

She told me, "Mr. Mays, we will take good care of your wife. We assigned her the best private room on the floor for her recovery. You can stay here as long as you want. Here is my business card with my home phone number on it. If you need anything, you call me at home personally."

Becky got her operation, and all went well. We only received a bill for twenty-nine dollars from an outside lab that did blood work or something. We gladly paid that bill as soon as we got it. God met our need because we remained faithful to Him.

Psalms 37:18 said, "The Lord takes care of those who obey Him, and the land will be theirs forever."

In September 1995, with about nine thousand dollars in our account, we headed to Panama to minister full-time to the Guaymi Indians. Willing to stay as long as God wanted, we had no idea how long we would live in this third world country.

We went with the attitude of "Let's see what God does and go with His flow."

We didn't put God on a timetable and were prepared to live in Panama for the rest of our life. Friends we met in Panama had lived and ministered in the Darien Jungle for over thirty-five years, Dennis and Jeanne Cook, founders of Vida Ministries. They had graduated from Rhema as well. We met them in a commuter airport as we waited for a flight from Panama City to David. We were drawn to them because we didn't see many Americans in the commuter airport in Panama.

When we flew into Panama City, Panama from the US, Enrique Sanchez met us at the airport. We stayed the night with him and his wife, Lupe. I informed Enrique that I needed a four-wheel drive Jeep for traveling in the mountains. I saved up some money in order to buy such a vehicle when we got to Panama. Enrique took us to a few dealerships. I found a used Jeep that I really liked. When I saw it, I knew that it would do just fine, no need to look elsewhere.

Enrique asked the dealer, "How much for that Jeep over there?"

The dealer replied, "I need nine thousand dollars for it."

Since the dealer spoke English well, I interjected, "I don't have that much money."

Insistent, the dealer wouldn't budge, so we talked a little while longer. He finally inquired, "How much would you pay for it?"

I generously replied, "I'll pay $7,500 for the Jeep."

The dealer scoffed excitedly, "I can't take that! I can tell you right now, I have a guy coming today who will pay nine thousand dollars for that vehicle. In reality, it's already sold. The buyer is coming later today to pay for it even though he hasn't put any money down yet."

Smiling, I declared, "Well, this is going to be my Jeep."

We haggled back and forth for a while.

Finally, the dealer asked, "What are you going to do with the Jeep?"

I replied, "I'm going to San Felix to feed Indian children there who are hungry and dying."

Moved with compassion, the dealer conceded, "Tell you what. I will let you have it for $7,500. How are you going to pay for it?"

I said, "Here is what I'm going to do. I'm going to give you $4,000 in cash right now and write you a check for $3,500."

He abruptly gasped. "No, I can't do that! It takes thirty days for a check to clear through the US, if it clears at all! Give me the $7,500 in cash now and you can have the jeep."

This compelled us to haggle for another thirty minutes.

Exasperated, the dealer said, "Look, I have a lot to do!" He called in his secretary and told her, "Make a copy of this man's passport. Get the $4,000 cash, the check for $3,500, and let him go."

We now had a Jeep to use for our missionary work.

Enrique and Lupe generously offered to let us stay rent free in their house in Boquete. Enrique at this time directed the Trinity

Broadcasting Network operations in Panama, so he and Lupe lived in a condominium in Panama City most of the time. Boquete, a small town with a Catholic church, an Assemblies of God church, and a Baptist church, sat about three hundred miles from Panama City.

Back in Tennessee, Trinity Christian Fellowship as well as several individual people supported our ministry monthly. We also continued to rent out our furnished house in Cross Plains. In total, we received about $1,500 a month. We had a secretary who worked out of one of the offices at Trinity Christian Fellowship. She collected the money, deposited it in the bank for us, and paid any bills. Down in Panama, I took out cash advances using my credit card for money to live and operate with. The secretary then paid the credit card bill when it came in.

Becky and I had travel visas that we needed to renew every three months by leaving Panama and then coming back. Boquete sat about an hour from the Costa Rica border. Every three months, Becky and I drove on Highway 1 to Paso Canoas, Costa Rica for the afternoon. When we returned to Panama, the border authority stamped our passports, and we were good for another three months. We did this routinely our entire tenure as full-time missionaries in Panama.

From Panama City, Becky and I loaded our new/used Jeep with the few belongings that we had and drove to Boquete. For the first six months or so, I spent most of my time with Moses, sharing the Gospel with the Indians in the mountains and helping him build a church building up there. Moses ultimately built two church buildings in the mountains near San Felix.

Sometimes Becky came with me up into the mountains. Finding it a hard trek which she didn't really like, she stayed at home and prayed for the ministry most of the time. Sometimes I traveled and preached revivals for a day or two. If I happened to be in Boquete on the weekend, we attended church at the Boquete Assemblies of God Church.

While Becky and I attended Bible school, a large Christian denomination took over the feeding center that we started with Marissa in San Felix. This denomination claimed ownership of the feeding center because it was in their *territory* and we were independent missionaries. Consequently, Marissa and her husband moved back to Panama City. Upon returning to Panama, we didn't fight the issue. Sadly, the feeding center closed because no one in this denomination truly had the compassionate heart to feed the poor.

In response, Moses and I established a feeding center higher up in the mountains where main denominations didn't want to go. They mainly ministered in the towns and cities. Moses got permission from the Panamanian authorities to use a room in a small school building up in the mountains to run a feeding center for the Indians.

Moses and I traveled in his three-quarter-ton truck to the big Chiquita banana processing plant in David. This plant had mounds and mounds of bananas that did not meet the specifications for shipment to the US. They called them cull bananas and just let them spoil. Moses got permission to haul them away while still fresh. We loaded up the truck with the cull bananas that were still good to eat and took them with us to the mountains to help feed the Indians. We did this several times. The mountains didn't have very many banana trees because most of them grew in the low lands on plantations.

Often, Moses took Becky and me to visit many people in their homes in Boquete and David. We spent the day with them sharing the Gospel and answering questions about God. We talked, fellowshipped, and prayed. Most of their prayer requests were health related. They also asked us to pray with them for loved ones. Moses gladly translated for us. We even met Manuel Noriega's aunt this way. On house arrest, she could go to church if she notified authorities. She attended the Assemblies of God Church in Boquete. One day, she invited us to her house for tea. She had a lovely house and seemed to be a very sweet lady. We visited her many times while we lived in Boquete.

From June through September 1996, we started doing revivals pretty much full-time, constantly on the go. We put eighteen thousand miles on the Jeep in that four-month period. I preached just about every day at these weeklong revivals. Sometimes I only preached one day at a certain location, but mostly I preached for an entire week. Enrique set up these engagements since he knew a multitude of pastors and ministers in Panama. Enrique also translated for me. If he couldn't go, then a younger man named Arturo accompanied me to do the interpreting. In addition, pastors referred me to their colleagues who then asked if I would come and do a revival at their church. When I didn't have any engagements scheduled, I went to the mountains with Moses for a few days and witnessed to the Indians one-on-one.

During these revivals, women brought boxes of clothes belonging to their loved ones for me to anoint. We saw many miracles happen through that. One didn't see these miracles happen much in the US because people didn't believe. But in Panama, people didn't have access to doctors and medical technology. Totally dependent on God, they believed. Also, we often saw the joy of the Lord fall on people, and they laughed uncontrollably during the service while I preached.

One of the first revivals, I did a weeklong engagement at the Boquete Assemblies of God Church. We started on Monday night teaching about the basics of salvation and the power of God to do miracles and healing. We taught this each night during the week. On the weekend, we had one service Saturday night and two on Sunday where God demonstrated His power and moved in miraculous ways because the people's faith built up.

Romans 10:17 said, "So then faith comes by hearing, and hearing by the word of God."

If people didn't know God's word, then they had little faith in the things of God. The Guaymi Indians grew up exposed to witchcraft and other dark practices that came from their indigenous religious beliefs.

The weekend had the largest attendance because the Indians lived and foraged in the mountains during the week and came into town on Friday, Saturday, and Sunday. This church had a lot of Guaymi Indians who attended service on the weekend. The revival service on Saturday didn't end until after midnight. The power of God moved strongly with uncontrollable laughter breaking out throughout the church.

The pastor, Ivan Gonzales, said, "Brother Herbie, we'll probably get in trouble with the police because we missed the midnight curfew."

Boquete had a midnight curfew where everyone had to be off the streets for the night. The police patrolled the town and enforced this curfew.

I told the pastor, "Just tell everyone that if they get stopped by the police, say that you've been at Joel's Place drinking."

I said this referencing Joel 2:28, "And afterward, I will pour out my Spirit on all people. Your sons and daughters will prophesy, your old men will dream dreams, your young men will see visions." This was because the Holy Spirit had moved powerfully at this revival.

When people left the service that night, they laughed hardily because they became drunk in the Spirit. I mean, they acted really loopy. As a consequence, a lot of people got stopped by the police in town.

The police questioned them, "Why are you out so late?"

They replied, "We have been drinking at Joel's place."

The police asked, "Where's Joel's place? We're not familiar with that establishment."

They responded, "It's the Assemblies of God Church."

The police retorted skeptically, "You have been drinking at church? What have you been drinking? Why were you there so late?"

They then told the police about the revival and what God had done. By Sunday morning, everyone knew of the revival. This occurrence proclaimed the power and love of God to the entire town.

During the revival service on Sunday morning, an Indian lady responded to the altar call and came up front. She told the interpreter, Arturo, that she wanted prayer for salvation. As she approached, I noticed that she had a different expression on her face than the rest of the people, an expression that I could only describe as a wicked contortion. I discerned that she had an evil spirit within her. I told Arturo that I would pray for her and cast that devil out of her. No sooner than I said that, the woman spat a stream of blood at me from between her two front teeth.

Then this uneducated Guaymi Indian lady from the mountains of Panama spoke perfect English to me, "You cannot cast the devil out of me!"

Irritated by the actions of this demon, I laid hands on her, and she fell to the floor under the power of God. She shook, convulsed, and rolled around on the floor for about ten or fifteen minutes. When she got up, that bizarre expression was no longer on her face. She then received salvation.

During the revival service on Sunday night, people packed the church to capacity. Expansion joints divided the concrete floor of the church into several sections, creating a series of lines on the floor, somewhat like the major yard lines on a football field. The Holy Spirit informed me that the power of God concentrated beyond the line near me there at the front of the church. When the people walked over that line, the power of God would touch and heal them. I repeated this to Arturo. As about two hundred people came forward and walked over the line, most fell under the power of God. I never touched them. The altar call took about two hours to do.

A mother came up with her eight- or nine-year-old little boy. She told Arturo that her son had an incurable heart disease. Maybe in the US the medical knowledge and technology to help him existed but not for the Panamanian Indians. I instructed Arturo to tell the mother to let the little boy walk toward us and step over the line. When he did, what looked like an imprint from an invisible finger started slowly making a circle on the boy's shirt around his heart as he stood there.

In amazement, Arturo exclaimed, "Look at the shirt! It's moving by itself!"

Then the little boy fell to the floor.

We did a twelve-day revival at the Assemblies of God Church in Caldera, Panama which sat about nine miles east of Boquete. The first night of the revival, the pastor told me that I would really be preaching to two different churches there. His congregation had split into two factions because of some family squabble within the church. Those who sat on the left fumed at those who sat on the right and had nothing to do with them. Those who sat on the right reciprocated, the most ridiculous thing I ever saw. During the revival, God moved in such mighty ways that by the end, the church united together with people hugging each other and crying.

About the sixth day of the revival, a lady came up front during the altar call. I thought her pregnant because she had a large round belly.

I asked Arturo, "What does she need God to do for her?"

After speaking with her momentarily, he told me, "This lady has had a tumor in her body for fourteen years. They cannot operate on it here in Panama. That's why her belly is bloated. She's not pregnant."

I called Becky over to lay hands on the lady's stomach. We prayed that God would heal her of this tumor. However, nothing happened for her that night at the service. By now, I learned not to take credit for what God did and not to take blame for what didn't happen.

The next night at the revival as we sang worship and praise songs to God, a skinny lady wearing a nice dress walked into the church.

I mentioned to Arturo, "That lady looks familiar."

Arturo replied, "Brother Herbie, I think she's the lady who had the stomach tumor that we prayed for last night."

I stepped up and told the music leader to stop the singing and had Arturo call the lady to the front.

Arturo asked, "Are you the lady that got prayed for with the tumor?"

She replied, "Yes."

Arturo said, "Please tell us what happened."

She explained, "After I got home from the revival service last night, I started having these pains in my stomach, so I started praising God. At midnight I passed the tumor out of my body through my bowels."

A great testimony for God in that town, everyone knew that she used to have a bloated belly from the tumor, but no longer!

When we started the revival for this church, I noticed on a display board that the church only took in around twenty-eight dollars for the previous month. The church only had this to operate on to include the pastor's salary. The pastor, his wife, and two children barely got by. Because of this, I preached every night on faith, giving, and believing on God.

A few days into the revival, I told the people, "If you don't have any money, I want you to bring a rock or anything else that you can offer to God and believe in faith that you are giving something to God."

So, they started bringing stuff. They brought bananas, coffee beans, rocks, and various stuff, as well as money to put in the offering. When the twelve days of revival concluded, the little church took in about $280, ten times the amount from last month.

The pastor came to me and said, "Brother Herbie, we want to give you eighty dollars out of the total money offering collected."

At first, I wanted to decline the money, but something slapped me upside the head and said, "You just spent two weeks teaching them to give in faith. Now that they want to sow a seed of generosity by giving out of their need, you want to sabotage their blessing. You have to receive their seed offering." So, I took the eighty dollars.

The first night of this revival, I noticed that their church building didn't have a roof on it. I declared to them, "By the time this revival ends, we will raise enough money to put a roof on your church building."

This would cost about $1,500 to purchase the metal, other material, and labor. Around the third day of the revival, I called the secretary of Trinity Christian Fellowship in White House, Tennessee who handled the money for my ministry.

She told me, "Brother Herb, this morning a lady came by and said that the Lord told her to put $1,500 in your missionary account."

That night at the revival service I told the people that we got the money for the roof. Disbelief and joy overwhelmed them at the same time. They had experienced a miracle from God. About a month later, a welder friend of mine came down from the US, and we put the roof on that little church building.

In a small community not far from David, we did a revival in a small church of about fifty people. We only did a Saturday night service at this church. During the altar call, a little boy came up and said that he wanted to get saved. As he approached the front, I noticed the same wicked contortion in his expression that the demon possessed lady of our first revival had. I told Arturo that I would not pray for his salvation unless his mamma or daddy approved. He informed me that they weren't there. I told the little boy through the interpreter that I wanted to speak with his parents first.

Suddenly, the little boy hissed and growled as he lunged toward me and scratched up my arm. A few men grabbed the boy and pulled him off me. Four grown men struggled to restrain this little boy and take him outside. After a while, he calmed down, they let him go, and he ran off. The pastor of that church told me that the little boy's parents worshipped the devil. He suspected that they sent the boy to the church that night to disrupt things.

During one of these revivals while Enrique interpreted for me, the Holy Spirit moved so powerfully that Enrique got baptized in the Holy Spirit while in the very act of translating for me. Instead of speaking Spanish, he spoke in tongues.

After that, Enrique often said after revival services, "Brother Herbie sure had the anointment tonight!"

During this season of revivals that God used us for, we worked nonstop, constantly on the go for four months. I now realized that the hard times and the deprivation that we endured during Bible school prepared us for such a time as this.

In 1996, I had the honor of being guest speaker at the national convention for the Church of God in Panama. Moses and Enrique came with me. Preachers, their wives, and church officials packed out the auditorium, totaling about a thousand people. I got up and preached the message with Enrique translating.

Afterward, the Holy Spirit told me in His silent voice, "I want to manifest Myself and show these people the power of God."

Even though Pentecostal, most of these attendees didn't operate in the gifts of the Holy Spirit. They didn't experience manifestations of God in their churches because of their lack of faith in such things.

The Holy Spirit further said, "Have a couple ushers stand behind the people that I point out to you. I am going to overwhelm them with My presence. Have the ushers catch them when they fall out."

I told Enrique what God wanted to do and then the audience, "The Holy Spirit wants to manifest His presence to you and show you His power. I'm going to stand here in the front and point people out one at a time. A couple of ushers will stand behind them, and the Holy Spirit will show His power."

Standing at the front of the auditorium, I called people out one at a time and had them go to the aisle where an usher stood behind them.

As the Lord lead me to a certain person, I called them out, "The lady in the red dress in the tenth row to the left, stand up and come to the aisle." When they did, I prayed, "Holy Spirit, touch them."

Each person fell out under the power and presence of God. The Holy Spirit did this for about an hour. The power of God moving like this surprised Enrique even though he had been working with me for a while and had seen stuff like this.

Afterward, a Church of God pastor asked Moses if I would come and preach at his church in the city of David. I agreed. Moses and Arturo came with me. The people who attended this church were a little more upscale in the social circles of David than those I normally preached to. At this time, I had four young men from Georgia who were brothers. Their last name was Frady. I called them the Frady Bunch. I met them when I preached in a church in Georgia. They wanted to come to Panama, so I arranged it. They came to David to assist me in helping Moses construct a church building up in the mountains for the Indians. They came to the service to assist us that night.

As I preached, the pastor and his wife sat way back to the side by themselves. Afterward, I did an altar call in which about fifty people came up front stretching from one side of the building to the other. I told the Frady brothers to stand behind them and catch them as they fell out. I wanted the Frady brothers to move down the line as I moved down the line praying for people. As I did, the Fradys never moved. I prayed for a lady who fell out on the concrete floor because no one caught her.

I said, "Come on. You got to move down the line with me."

They replied, "Brother Herbie, we can't move our feet. They're stuck to the floor. We literally cannot move!"

Moses and a couple other men came up and helped me pray for the rest of the people, while the Frady brothers remained stuck standing in the same spot the entire time.

Meanwhile, the pastor and his wife rolled around on the floor in the back of the church. Sometime during the altar call, the power of God fell on them too. After the service, we got in the Jeep and pulled out of the parking lot.

Moses sheepishly confessed, "Brother Herbie, this pastor is really going to be mad. I didn't tell you before the service, but he tried to set you up. He invited you to preach at his church to prove that what you did at the convention was fake."

The next day, Moses informed me that this pastor wanted to see me. I agreed to meet with him.

With tears streaming down his face, he said, "I want to repent for mocking the power of God. I tempted God when I invited you to preach at my church. I shouldn't have done that. This stuff is real."

I found out a long time ago that God can do whatever He wants, even make a believer out of a skeptic any time He chooses.

One day, I attended a big cookout at Enrique's house in Panama City. A pastor of a church there asked Enrique if I would preach at the dedication service of their new sanctuary building. I gladly accepted. This young man started a church in his apartment in the rough part of Panama City with the motto, "Tell one, win one." He started out with five people and asked each one to witness to others until they persuaded one person to attend the church. As each member did this, the church grew to more than a thousand members. After five years, the church flourished and moved into a new building in 1996. I got to preach at the dedication service which the Trinity Broadcasting Network in Panama televised.

Around September of 1996, the revivals started to slow down. I felt change coming to our ministry and that God would soon move us in another direction. The neighborhood where we lived formed a giant loop. In the morning, I walked this loop while I prayed.

In so doing one morning in October, God spoke to me in His silent voice, "I want you to go to Portland, Tennessee and build Me a church there and love the people through the power of the Holy Spirit. I want you to allow Me to exhibit My presence through the Holy Spirit in that place."

I knew little about Portland and had only been there a few times. My daughter lived just outside this little town. We passed by it on our way to visit her, but we didn't go into Portland. I liked missionary work and didn't want to be a pastor. I told Becky what God had said.

I confided in her, "Becky, I don't want to be a pastor, but I believe God wants us to go to Portland and start a church there."

Lately, Becky also had a stirring in her that some kind of change was imminent. She responded, "Well, that's what we need to do then."

I had a long conversation with God. "I really don't want to do this. If this is a success, it will be because of You, not because of me. I don't want to go, and I'm not going to help you a lot. I'll go and do it, but I am not happy about it."

I felt this way because I really enjoyed mission work, the revivals, watching the power of God bless downtrodden people, and traveling to different places. I experienced some unforgettable times, the memories of which I relished for the rest of my life.

CHAPTER 11

A New Frontier

We left Panama in November 1996 and returned to Tennessee with forty-two dollars in our pocket and no employment. The house we owned had tenants living in it who were three months behind on the rent. They knew that as missionaries we could return at any time in which they would have to vacate. They agreed to this arrangement. We contacted them about two weeks before returning to the US. They found another place to live by the time we got back to Tennessee, but never paid us the three months back rent. We just let it go.

I contacted contractors that I knew and started painting again to earn money. I got in touch with friends that I used to go to church with who currently didn't attend any specific church. I told these three families about the church that I would pioneer in Portland. Interested in that prospect, they joined us in late November, as we started out meeting on Sunday morning at someone's house. We did a little Bible study and talked about how to start the new church.

After getting settled in from our return to Tennessee, I got in the car and drove up to Portland. I saw this little storefront building on the corner for sale near city hall. With its dimensions about thirty by forty feet, it offered roughly twelve hundred square feet of space along with a few offices. I figured it was as good a place as any to start out. The lady who owned the building lived in Madison.

I called her and asked, "How much are you asking for the building?"

She replied, "I want sixty-five thousand dollars for it. I'll meet you at the building tomorrow to show you around."

The following day, we met at the storefront.

She told me, "I have owned this building for a long time. I'm getting old and now want to sell it. What are you going to use the building for?"

I replied, "Well, I'm going to start a church in here."

Smiling at me graciously, she said, "If you're going to put a church in this building, then you can have it for sixty thousand dollars."

To which I gladly replied while projecting an air of confidence, "Okay, I'm going to take it." All the while, I fretted over the fact that I only had forty-two dollars cash to my name.

I went to see a banker at the Bank of Goodlettsville that I did business with when I owned the paint and carpet stores. I greeted him warmly and explained, "Tim, I want to buy a building up in Portland. It's sixty thousand dollars. I need to borrow the entire amount. I'm going to use the building to start a church."

He replied, "Herb, we have done a lot of business over the years, a lot. You have always paid me back on time. Because of that, I'm going to do my best to get you a loan for sixty thousand dollars. I know you won't disappoint me. Go on up there and make a success of it."

We purchased the little storefront property using equity in our house and the value of the new property as collateral. In the middle of the town of Portland, we started the church. I owned the building and leased it to the church for the cost of the mortgage. We never had any trouble making the payment on time. We renovated the building, painting, as well as put in new carpet. I told Becky and even God that I didn't want to be a pastor. However, I submitted to God knowing that He would be the One to make it a success.

While cleaning our new little building, I discovered two broken window panes, so I went to the glass company next door, which a couple who lived in Portland owned. I asked the wife, "Can I get two glass panes cut? We just bought the building next store."

Intrigued, she replied, "Oh, what are you doing with the building?"

Sticking my chest out, I proudly answered, "We're going to start a church there."

She lectured back, "Oh gosh, we don't need another church in Portland. We've got plenty of churches in this town." She then inquired, "What kind of church is it?"

Smiling gleefully, I replied, "Well, it's a Pentecostal, Holy Ghost church. We're going to let the Holy Spirit move and touch people's lives with the power of God."

Waving her hand dismissively, she quipped, "Oh, that will never catch on here!"

That ended my glee and the conversation about the new church. We then processed my order for the two window panes.

A few days later, her husband stopped by for a chat. He went to one of the denominational churches in town. He served as pastor for their satellite church across town. He told me that, in reality, the satellite church existed for the people that the big regular church didn't want in their services. He ministered to the people that weren't welcomed at the main church.

I thought, "My goodness! I can't believe that a church would do such a thing!"

Despite this bumpy start, the three of us became good friends, for they were good Christians who genuinely loved people. Months later, a man and his family started attending our church for a few years until they moved away. He told me about his first time at that same denominational church.

An usher met him at the door and decreed, "If you come back next week, you need to have a tie on."

On January 12, 1997, we held our first service in the new building with about twelve people in attendance, including Lesley and my granddaughter. We had little space heaters spread about the sanctuary to battle the bitter frigid air of that icy morning. Eventually, we installed central heat and air. We started the church completely leaning on God. I didn't advertise, go door to door, or witness to anyone.

I put a simple vinyl sign over the front door that said, "Hosanna Church, A Spirit-Filled Fellowship."

I always liked the word *Hosanna* because it meant "God save us!" People started to trickle in a few here, a few there. A church that gave the Holy Spirit complete freedom to do what He wanted, people experienced the powerful move of God at Hosanna Church.

I didn't take a salary, so I continued painting houses to earn money. We never hounded people about money donations to the church. Despite that, the church never struggled financially. Our policy was to pay bills as soon as we received them and to have three to four months' worth of our budget in the bank at all times. Two years later, the trustee board told me that the church took in enough money to pay me three hundred dollars a week as the pastor.

During the autumn of our first year, I arrived early to the church one Sunday morning. Sitting in my office drinking coffee, I saw a car slowly, almost hesitantly, pull up in front of the building and stop. A man, woman, and little girl sat motionless inside. The man timidly got out of the car, a blank expression on his face. The woman and little girl stayed in the car still and quiet, covered by a shroud of depression which stole all joy and hope. When the man walked into the church, I first noticed a pungent smell about him. He entered my office and introduced himself. In addition to the strong odor, dirt and grime covered him.

He said meekly, "Preacher, I work at the stockyards in Lafayette. I got paid this week and used all my money to pay the rent. I don't have any money left to buy food for my wife and my little girl. I was wondering if you could give me some money."

We talked for a while.

Then I said, "I don't have any money in the church. We don't keep any money here."

We continued to talk. We must have talked for about thirty minutes total.

Finally, I said, "Tell you what, I'm going to give you money from myself." I reached into my pocket, pulled out about thirty or forty dollars, and gave it to him. "Here, this is all I've got on me."

Sitting at the desk across from me, the man accepted the money and replied, "If you let me, I will come back this week and work this off."

I responded, "No, you don't have to do that."

He went on to further say, "Well, can I pray for you then?"

This impressed me because most people looking for a handout don't offer to pray for you. He reached out, grabbed my hand, and prayed. Billy Graham in all his years never prayed a prayer as moving as that man did just then. The presence of God entered that office as I received an anointed prayer from this vagabond person. The man and his family left. I never saw them again. Afterward, I felt that his visit was godsent. I believed that God divinely appointed that man to show up at the church that morning.

A little while later, the church service started at eleven o'clock. About sixty people sitting on folding chairs packed into our little sanctuary. When the singing and worship ended, I got up to preach. Suddenly, a wind rushed in from the side door and swept through the building. As the wind moved from one side of the sanctuary to the other, the power of God knocked everyone down like a wave. I never preached that morning. My recollection of the rest of the service remained foggy as we reveled in the presence of God for a time. After the service, Becky and I drove home in separate cars.

My mind not on driving but on what happened that morning, I spoke to God, "Lord, I just don't understand how You could come and do that, Your presence so strong today in that church. Thank You, God, for doing that."

God replied, "If you hadn't fed the man and his family this morning, I couldn't have moved during the church service."

Pondering this, I continued to praise God in an attitude and atmosphere of worship oblivious to the world around me. Suddenly, a thump jolted me as I hit the back of Becky's car because she stopped at a Stop sign. Fortunately, it didn't do much damage.

Shortly after this, God touched the life of a three-year-old girl in the church. She had a tumor on her backside. Scheduled for an operation on Monday, her parents brought her to the altar that Sunday for prayer. We laid hands on that precious baby and prayed. The next day, the tumor was gone, having disappeared sometime during the night. This little girl's grandparents still attend our church.

Our building could only hold about sixty people. Within six months, we had standing-room only during services lasting for three hours because of the strong presence of God. We had long altar calls because God moved in mighty ways. God's strong presence inhabited the sanctuary so that nobody wanted to leave. Therefore, we stayed and sang praise and worship for over an hour after the end of the services.

A man who was the Sunday school superintendent of a denominational church here in Portland dated a lady who attended our church. He heard about the moves of God at our services and wanted to experience it for himself. One Sunday morning after tending to his duties at his church, he came to our service that started at eleven o'clock. He responded to the altar call that morning and fell under the power of God. After the service ended, people had to physically carry him out of the building, put him in a car, and take him home. Shortly after that, he resigned his position at the other church and started attending Hosanna Church.

In this book, I made mention several times of people falling out under the power of God. This occurred because the human flesh cannot endure the awesome power of God Almighty. The Bible referenced this in the following passages:

1. Revelation 1:12–17: "Then I turned to see the voice that spoke with me. And having turned I saw seven gold lampstands, and in the midst of the seven lampstands One like the Son of Man, clothed with a garment down to the feet and girded about the chest with a golden band. His head and hair were white like wool, as white as snow, and His eyes like a flame of fire; His feet were like fine brass, as if refined in a furnace, and His voice as the sound of many

waters; He had in His right hand seven stars, out of His mouth went a sharp two-edged sword, and His countenance was like the sun shining in its strength. When I saw Him, I fell at his feet as though dead. Then he placed His right hand on me and said: 'Do not be afraid. I am the First and the Last.'"

2. Mathew 28:2–4: "And behold, there was a great earthquake; for an angel of the Lord descended from heaven, and came and rolled back the stone from the door, and sat on it. His countenance was like lightning, and his clothing as white as snow. And the guards shook for fear of him, and became like dead men."

3. Ezekiel 1:28: "Like the appearance of a rainbow in a cloud on a rainy day, so was the appearance of the brightness all around it. This was the appearance of the likeness of the glory of the Lord. So when I saw it, I fell on my face and heard a voice of One speaking."

4. Daniel 8:16–18: "And I heard a man's voice between the banks of the Ulai, who called, and said, 'Gabriel, make this man understand the vision.' So he came near where I stood, and when he came I was afraid and fell on my face; but he said to me, 'Understand, son of man, that the vision refers to the time of the end.' Now, as he was speaking with me, I was in a deep sleep with my face to the ground; but he touched me and stood me upright."

Another person touched by Hosanna Church, Josh, a teenage drug addict, hung around the neighborhood with his friends. They stood on the corner by the church. The biggest drug dealer in town lived at the other end of the street. One Sunday morning, they walked into the service, about five of them. They had earrings, body piercings, tattoos, and chains hanging from their clothes, very thuggish looking. A few weeks later, they came back again. Within a few months, all of them received salvation and started bringing in other teenagers. I didn't have a youth pastor at the time, so I did a youth service with them on Sunday nights. Becky even bought me a chain to hang from my clothes like them. We ended up having a good youth group of about twenty.

A few years later, Josh served as an usher in the church. The usher jackets hung on a coat rack in the corner of my office. One Sunday morning, I sat in my office having a pity party because I had a bad week. I didn't want to preach. I didn't want to do anything that morning.

When Josh came in to get his usher coat, he turned to me and said, "Pastor Herb, can I tell you something? When you started this church in Portland, I was on drugs and carried a gun. If you hadn't started this church, I'd be dead today. I just want to thank you for loving me and coming to Portland."

Needless to say, that ended my pity party.

Through the years, God touched a lot of lives using Becky and me in ministry. Young people like Josh didn't need to hear how bad they were because they already knew. They grew up in broken homes where some didn't even know their daddy. Those that did never saw their daddy much anyway. Most of the kids in the youth group came from this background. Becky and I gave them the one thing they needed most—love. Unfortunately, we didn't win them all, but we had more successes than not.

In the latter part of 1997, a lady who attended our church brought a missionary named Gladstone Fairweather to my office one day. People called him Brother Stoney. We formed a strong friendship right away. Two missionaries adopted him as a twelve-year-old boy in Jamaica. He lived and received his education in the US. He had worked as hospital administrator for Meharry Medical College in Nashville. Now, he lived in Jamaica as a missionary and founded a Bible school and seven churches there. Around 1998, we began supporting his ministry financially. Once a year, I traveled to Jamaica to do a revival for him during his annual camp meeting.

Brother Stoney owned a plot of land in Jamaica that a lady donated on which to build himself a house. At this time, the Fairweathers rented.

In 2005, as we walked by the piece of land, Brother Stoney said, "I've raised a little bit of money. But someday, I will have enough to build a house there."

I complained, "Brother Stoney, I've been coming here for years now. Each time, we pass by this piece of property and you state that you are going to build a house there. But I see no progress. In fact, the land is kind of overgrown." I continued, "Let me ask you a question. Do you have a bricko-block?"

Brother Stoney answered, "Well yeah, I have some bricko-blocks at the church."

I then said, "Okay, when we get back to your house, we'll go to the church and get one bricko-block. And then, we are going to bring it and put it on this land. Now, every morning when you walk by, you thank God that your house is there. You identify that one bricko-block as your house."

Brother Stoney gave me an odd look, thinking my suggestion peculiar. Nevertheless, I got a commitment from him to do it, which he did for three years.

In 2008, he called me and said, "Brother Herb, I have architectural plans to build a house and would like you to look at it."

I agreed to Brother Stoney's request. He made a visit to Tennessee that year in July. We took his plans to a contractor in Nashville, Joe M. Rogers, who had previously helped Brother Stoney build a church. Joe looked at the plans and donated money to help build the house. Next, I put a forty-foot shipping container in the parking lot of our church in Portland and stored purchased and donated items in it like hurricane windows, floor tile, etc. In addition to filling up the entire trailer, we raised thirty thousand dollars from various donors in about a year. Our church in Portland matched that with another thirty thousand dollars to pay for building Brother Stoney's house.

We got the container shipped free of charge from the US to Jamaica through Averitt Express. In addition to this, Brother Stoney knew someone who worked in the office of one of our senators. They issued us a letter asking the Jamaican government to waive all duty fees and taxes. As a result, we shipped the materials for Brother Stoney's house into Jamaica free of charge as well. Once the storage container arrived in Kingston, Jamaica, we had difficulty getting it released by the customs department. After intricate negotiations with one of the customs agents, we finally got the container released. From there, we moved it to Brother Stoney's land in Trelawny Parish.

Rules didn't allow us to remove the lock from the container until customs inspectors arrived to match the contents with the manifest. Two lady inspectors arrived on a hot, sweltering day. Infernally hateful toward us, they demanded that each item be taken out of the container, verified against the manifest, documented on a customs form, assigned a value, and duty paid based on the value. Barking orders and snarling directives at us, they declared that this would take several days. Brother Stoney and his wife, Sister Evelyn, withered under the heavy heat of anxiety.

They fretted, "Brother Herb, these people are going to charge us thousands of dollars for this stuff!"

After some more intricate negotiations, the two inspectors signed off on the paperwork and left without charging anything.

The building of the Fairweather's house proved an arduous undertaking because each stage of the process required inspection and the approval signature of a government official. Actual construction took well over a year. In 2010, we finally finished the project. The Fairweathers moved in and had a beautiful house overlooking the ocean.

Having built houses in the past, I knew that this was fairly achievable. Brother Stoney, on the other hand, struggled to see such a reality because he had no knowledge of how to build houses or the finances to pay for it. The entire endeavor seemed like an unsurmountable mountain to him in the beginning. I got great satisfaction in helping him since he did so much for the kingdom of God. I was honored to have the opportunity to help.

I was also honored to do tent revivals for Brother Stoney. At the first one that we did, people packed into the service.

Two Jamaican girls sang the chorus that goes, "I see the Lord. He is high and lifted up. And His train fills the temple. And the angels cry holy. The angels cry holy. The angels cry holy is the Lord."

Those two precious little girls sounded like a couple of angels themselves. A great anointing materialized during that song. Immeasurably impressed with this anointing, I beseeched the two girls to keep singing that song. We sang it for what seemed like an hour.

In the midst of all this, a paralyzed man named Mr. Beckworth sat at the back of the tent. Paralyzed on one side due to a stroke, he had difficulty walking and only raised one hand in worship to God. Suddenly, he stood up and started walking toward the front of the service with both hands raised to God. Then he began jumping around the tent, rejoicing.

Everybody in this community knew of his paralysis and saw him jumping about. At this point, everybody in the revival let loose a torrent of praise to God. Then people started falling out under the power of God.

During my later trips to Jamaica, Mr. Beckworth came up to me and declared, "I still have my miracle! I can still walk!"

He eventually moved back to England. What a testimony that must have been for his family and friends in that country, as well!

Later we held another revival in Wakefield, Jamaica. A man stood outside the church with a switchblade knife, intimidating people as they came in. The town had a lot of devil worshippers and witchcraft. As we sang the praise and worship, many at the revival sat in fear because of the man out front. I got up to preach but couldn't say anything meaningful or coherent. I felt an immense heaviness bear down on me. I struggled just to move and had difficulty getting my thoughts together. I heard myself speak, but the words fell flat to the floor like chunks of lead.

I thought to myself, "Well, something is wrong here!"

I told the people to sing another song. As they did, the heavy weight intensified throughout the church. We struggled just to do anything.

Finally, I dismissed the people from the service for that night and promised them, "I'm going to fast and pray. I'll be back tomorrow night and I'll be spiritually ready."

Back at Brother Stoney's house, I began to pray. I still felt the heaviness. Then the Holy Spirit told me that devil worshippers put a spell on the revival, resulting in a spiritual hinderance, something difficult to believe if never experienced. Because of this, I fasted and prayed until the heaviness lifted away. Once we confronted the hinderance with spiritual weapons, it left.

The following night, we gathered at the church. The devil-worshipping man with the knife resumed his efforts outside of the church. After the congregation sang a few songs, I took my Bible, walked through the front doors of the church, and stood defiantly on the porch, glaring at the knife-wielding man.

Waving my Bible at him as a weapon, I declared, "I curse you and bind you in the name of Jesus!" The man took off running. The revival flourished for the rest of the week as numerous people got saved and rededicated to God.

We saw a lot of people saved in Jamaica rather than healed like our experience in Panama. The Jamaican people lived in fear of witchcraft and other spiritual evil. Our revivals there tended to give them courage that belonging to God protected them from all that stuff. The Holy Spirit knew what the Jamaican people needed most.

Brother Stoney told me, "Brother Herb, these Jamaicans really like you because you're the only white man that comes over here from the US and preaches like a black man."

Traveling to and preaching in Jamaica blessed us because of the good and wonderful Jamaican people.

CHAPTER 12

Building Upon Foundations

Back in Portland, we outgrew our current sanctuary and needed a bigger place. We planned on expanding our current building but couldn't get a permit due to parking constraints around the building.

I told a friend who attended our church, "We want to buy a piece of property beyond the city limits out in the county to build a new church sanctuary on."

He informed me, "There is a piece of land for sale just down the highway from the market I work at."

I went to look at the land and speak with the owner. The lady who owned the property said we could buy the twenty-one acres of land for eighty-nine thousand dollars. She and her husband intended to build a house there but changed their mind when he suddenly had a heart attack. I accepted the offer and asked Tim at the bank for a loan, which got approved using the value of the land as collateral.

Come to find out, the husband previously turned down an offer from a local dentist to buy that same property for $125,000. Unaware of this and her name on the property deed, she sold the land to us for $36,000 less in the autumn of 1998. Her husband later stopped by and teased me about all that.

He declared with a grin, "So, you're the man who stole my property!"

We then chatted pleasantly for a while.

Shortly thereafter, we began clearing and preparing the ground to construct our first building on the new property. We poured the foundation that following spring. At that time, a ministry called Feed the Children received numerous heating/air-conditioning units from a donor in California. This ministry in turn donated units to a food bank in White House to do with whatever they wanted. That food bank donated four heating/air-conditioning units for our new building. We paid nothing.

In addition, an electrical contractor came in and did all the electrical work free for us as well. The project took over a year to complete. In December 1999, we held our first service in the new sanctuary on the new property right before Y2K. (Anyone remember that?) I rented the old storefront building to a small group of people who wanted to start a Pentecostal church. They experienced the baptism in the Holy Spirit and had to leave the denominational church that they currently attended because of that. After a year, they bought the building from me.

Around 2004, we added to the new church building a fellowship hall with a two-bedroom apartment on the back end for Becky and me to live in. Around 2008, we started constructing an addition to the building for a youth room. After we laid the foundation, we planned to build it further as we raised the money to pay for it. We only had about a thousand dollars in the building fund and had to strive to raise that. During one of our Saturday night prayer meeting, I sat against the wall, praying for funding to complete this project.

The Lord told me in His silent voice, "Go into your office and get a check. Write out the amount that you want in order to build the youth room."

I walked into my office, got a blank check from the church checkbook, and wrote the amount of fifty thousand dollars made out to "cash". Then I put the check in my desk, believing in faith that we would get that amount.

About a month later as I ran errands in town, Becky called me from our apartment, which adjoined the back end of the church.

"There are some people here that want to speak with you," she said.

I returned to the apartment and greeted the people, a man and his wife who used to attend the church. We talked for a while.

Then he said, "We have something that we want to give you to help build the youth room." Turning to his wife, he said with a big smile, "Honey, why don't you show him?"

She proceeded to present to me fifty thousand dollars! They asked, "Do you think that will cover it?"

Engulfed in a surreal moment, I replied, "Yes! I think that should do it."

We prayed God's blessing upon them, and they left.

Later, I thought to myself, "You big dummy! When God told you to write out that check for whatever amount you wanted, you should have put a million dollars!"

Two months later, with the project almost completed, our generous donor called and asked me to swing by his house. When I did, he gave me another ten thousand dollars for good measure, saying, "Here's a little extra to help you finish the youth room."

During this time, a couple from Westmorland named Dwayne and Niecy attended the church. Their little daughter had an incurable skin disease which gave her skin a scaly, rough appearance like that of an alligator. One Sunday morning, the Holy Spirit did an altar call for healing. They brought their little girl up in response. We anointed her with oil and prayed for her to have healthy skin. The next day, as Niecy bathed her daughter, all the scaly skin and scabs washed off. Niecy had to use a strainer to keep it from clogging the drain. From that day forward, her daughter had baby soft skin. Niecy wrote a letter to the national organization, advocating on behalf of those with this incurable disease and told them that a cure did indeed exist, the healing touch of God.

Another time, my son-in-law cut his finger while working with a power saw. Even though the doctor sewed the finger back on, it remained locked in a curled position permanently. The doctor said he could do nothing about it. One Sunday morning, my son-in-law sat in the balcony with Lesley while I preached.

As he looked down at me standing at the front of the church, he exclaimed, "Lesley, look at your daddy! There's a white aura all around him!"

Lesley replied, "I don't see anything."

Not a spiritual man, he insisted, "I'm telling you, there is something all white around him!"

Lesley again said, "Well, I don't see anything."

Suddenly his finger popped out straight and he could use it normally again. It completely healed.

Another instance, a lady named Beth Wilkinson had a tumor on her neck. She came to church one Sunday morning with the X-ray that showed the unwanted growth. We prayed for her. She went back to the doctor's office a few days later for a pre-operation X-ray which revealed that the tumor disappeared. It completely dissolved, so she never underwent surgery. Ever since, I enjoyed teasing her about having a goiter on her neck. She in turn scolded me because to her a goiter sounded much more atrocious than a tumor.

Around 2008, a man named Roger Johnson was diagnosed with cancer and given six months to live. He attended a church in White House at the time. He informed his pastor of the situation during Sunday service and requested prayer.

The pastor merely responded, "We'll put you on the prayer list."

After the service, Roger complained to his wife, "I'm dying of cancer and only have six months to live! All they're going to do is put me on a list! I'm going to Pastor Herb's church. At least they will lay hands on me and genuinely pray."

When Roger arrived at the church, he explained his situation to me. We gladly prayed the prayer of agreement with him. Then I encouraged him to continually make positive confessions about his healing regardless of any symptoms. After a year, all indications of cancer disappeared.

Ministry wasn't always rosy. We had our share of people leave the church for silly reasons. We saw many people get their life touched by God, then later leave the church offended over something petty. I heard it said that ministry would be all right except for the people.

One lady attended our church for about seven years. I preached her mother's funeral. We ministered to her when she had needs. We fellowshipped with her and fed her spiritually.

One day she wrote me a letter, "Brother Herb, I'm going to leave the church because for the past two weeks, you didn't speak to me after the service. I don't know what I did to you to deserve that."

Truth be told, at the end of services, I focused on speaking with new visitors. It wasn't feasible to get around to everybody in the church and speak to them personally after every service.

Another time, we invited a lady evangelist to speak at our church after she had asked a few times in the past if she could. That particular Sunday morning during praise and worship, a young woman walked in about ten minutes into the service and sat in the first row. I had never seen her before. I already gave the lady evangelist the cordless microphone as she sat ready to go. The young woman meanwhile began to cry uncontrollably.

I went over to console her and asked, "What's going on?"

She replied, "I'm going to have an abortion tomorrow. I don't know why I came to this church today. I just did. But, tomorrow, I'm going to kill my baby."

I gently told her, "No, you're not going to kill your baby tomorrow." I stopped the music and the singing and announced, "This morning, the church is going to intercede in prayer for a baby."

We spent the rest of the service praying for this young woman and her baby. People gathered around and prayed, while the worship team led the rest of the congregation in singing. As a result, the lady evangelist never got to preach.

After the service, I apologized to her, "I'm sorry, but today we just had to go in another direction. The church will go ahead and give you five hundred dollars for being here this morning and we'll have you back another time to minister."

Later that week, I received a scathing letter from the lady evangelist scolding me for missing God, calling me a disgrace, and that she had a specific message from God for my people that morning and I blew it.

About three months later, I got a call while in my office at the church, "Pastor Mays, I don't know if you remember me or not. I was the young woman who was going to have an abortion, but something made me go to your church that Sunday morning. Could you and your wife come visit me at the Gallatin hospital? I just gave birth to a little girl."

Overwhelmed to tears, I thought how much God loved the young woman and her unborn baby that He compelled her to pull into our church while driving down the highway and changed the flow of the service just for her. And so, a ten-year-old child lived out in the world somewhere because of the power and love of God.

Ironically, that lady evangelist repeatedly requested to speak at our church again after sending me that letter. Needless to say, we never extended her another invitation.

A similar incident, we invited a representative of the Gideons International to speak at our church in 2017.

As he and I chatted in my office before Sunday service, Roger Johnson walked in teary-eyed and said in a choked voice, "Last week, I had a brain scan which revealed a large tumor behind my eye." Cancer free for nine years, Roger went in for a checkup, because he experienced a painful sensation with his eyes. Unknown to him at the time, he had inadvertently used the wrong eyedrops, resulting in severe irritation. Consequently, the tumor was discovered.

After praise and worship, I called Roger to the front of the church, and we prayed with him. He fell out under the power of God. Then the Holy Spirit told me to open up the altar to anyone who needed prayer. In so doing, several people came up for prayer and fell out under the power of God, while the congregation sang praise and worship to God. Wide-eyed, the Gideons representative wasn't used to this kind of church service. Afterward, I encouraged Roger to continue making positive confessions about his healing from cancer.

Because God moved in a different direction that morning, the Gideons representative didn't speak. I apologized to him and gave him five hundred dollars for being there that morning.

Finding this whole experience wonderous, he declared, "Of all the churches that I have visited over the years all around the world, I never felt the presence of God as strongly as I did this morning. It's refreshing to see a church allow God to move however He wants to."

The following week, Roger had another brain scan which only showed a small spot on his brain, which his doctor treated with one dose of radiation. The doctor assured Roger that this treatment would resolve the issue and not to worry.

In September 2013, we changed the name of the church to the River at Portland. I always liked that name for a church too.

I had two sayings that correlated to this name: "When the Holy Spirit flows, go with the flow" and "If you stand on a wet river bank long enough, eventually you'll slip in."

If people attended the River at Portland Church long enough, eventually they had a spiritual encounter with God. In addition, I was always fond of rivers and creeks. So, it made sense to me to use such a name for the church.

Every now and then, God had me preach about finances. One Sunday morning in late fall of 2017, I preached on a message unrelated to finances. Then the Holy Spirit told me to do an altar call for wallets. He had me encourage people to support God's kingdom financially and to give any money collected at the altar call to Bridges, a homeless ministry in Nashville.

I told the congregation, "If you are not a tither, come up and put something in the offering plate. Give something to God. Then we will pray for your finances. We will give the entire offering collected here to Bridges."

We collected $530 from that altar call. Then I had those who gave hold up their wallets, and I prayed for them. At the end, one lady testified that when we prayed for wallets like this a few years ago, her monthly social security draw increased $1,300.

Our average donations received each week ran about $3,500. This particular Sunday, tithes and offerings that we took up at the beginning of the service hit $5,276.

After the service, a young lady approached me and said, "Pastor, I didn't put my tithe check in at the beginning of the service."

Inspired to support God's kingdom, she handed me a check for almost two hundred dollars. She and her husband had not been donating and had a wonderful breakthrough of faith that morning. Not trusting God financially made it difficult to trust God in all other areas of life.

The anointing of the Holy Spirit helped people trust God with their finances and give generously toward the homeless. Over the years, we saw the Holy Spirit move like this not only concerning finances, but in healing, in dealing with life's problems, in encouragement, in meeting needs, in whatever. Unfortunately, too many churches hindered God with their doubt and unbelief. In addition, people sat in church with their mind on what they will eat for lunch or wondering if they'll get home in time for the ballgame instead of focusing on God. I myself had done the same before I got saved.

Recently, during Pastor Appreciation Month, I received the following letter from one of the teenagers in the church named Ryan Carrion. He started attending church here about two years ago at the age of fourteen. He never spoke to anyone because he stuttered severely. The first time he sat in my office, he answered me in grunts. I quickly put an end to that and insisted that he at least try to talk to me if we were to have conversations. Since then, Ryan made good progress with his speech. His letter read,

> To commence with, I just need to say that I appreciate you with all my heart, Pastor. I knew I was a disaster when I came into this church that God and you put together, and I did not think I would be accepted there. In an instant I noticed something. Within a week, we were talking, laughing, and you treated me as your own. You're the only person who is able to make me happy just by being around you, because you took the effort to drop *everything* you were doing, *everything*, just to make me feel like I'm worth something to you. There are no words to possibly describe how much I love and greatly appre-

ciate you. I'm thankful for everything you have done for me whether it be talking to me, inviting me over, working with me, or even teaching me about God. Not only are you the most enthusiastic, wild preacher, you are also a huge inspiration. Every day God's presence is engulfing you, and He is using you for His will. I've been around you so much I can't stand not having what God gave you. I need to be Little Herbie or something. The point is that you made me who I am, a godly, happy young man. Everyone in this church appreciates you, especially since you are great as our shepherd and our friend. Everything you have done for me I kept inside my heart, and I will give back all the love you demonstrated to me. Pastor, I just wanted to say I love you and thank you for always being there for me! I couldn't live without you. You are my role model, and never give up on what you do. If that happens, let Little Herbie take care of it. I really appreciate you, Pastor Herb.

Over the past twenty years of having a church in Portland, Tennessee, we saw God do marvelous things. During this time, the church grew to an average of one hundred thirty people. Typical attendance at Sunday service hovered at about a hundred. God blessed us for being faithful in coming to Portland and starting a Spirit-filled church here. We made no apology for the move of the Holy Spirit and always gave God the freedom to do what he wanted in our church.

In contrast, a small church nearby didn't allow the Holy Spirit to move freely or believe in things like divine healing. Because that church didn't teach healing scriptures, its members lacked faith in

God's healing power. Consequently, they seemed to regularly visit one person or another from their congregation in the hospital.

Referencing this scripture once again, Romans 10:17 said, "So then faith comes by hearing, and hearing by the word of God."

At the River of Portland Church, we constantly talked about and believed in healing. Seldom did we have one of our own in the hospital.

Sunday services where the Holy Spirit moved and blessed hurting people spiritually and physically justified our ministry even though we only had about a hundred people in attendance. In the natural, people tended to consider churches with big crowds a success. It was never about the size of the crowd but always about allowing God to move during the service and touch hurting people. Jesus did that during His ministry. He blessed hurting people and taught them how to have a closer relationship with Father-God. No one could put a price on people getting saved or healed. It was about a person or a family getting what they needed from God that day. That defined ministry for me. I developed an appreciation for pastoring over the years and now had no regrets.

One of my profound realizations over the past twenty years was that a great church didn't require a great amount of people. Small churches could be great churches if they allowed God to move as He wanted. Quality of ministry exceeded quantity of followers. Anyone could draw a large crowd with a cookout but would merely feed the flesh not the spirit. Numbers meant little compared to nourishing the spirit and changing lives for the better. Jesus came to give us life more abundantly (John 10:10). We positively touched a myriad of lives in three countries over the past twenty-seven years by submitting to God, doing what He wanted us to do, and reaching the people that He wanted us to reach.

CHAPTER 13

Breaching the Wall Within Me

After a time here in Portland, a very nice man named Terry who attended the church knew that I had served in Vietnam. He beseeched me, "Pastor, I want you to go to the Vietnam Veterans Memorial in Washington, D.C. It will do you good to visit the wall there. You'll get closure."

I said, "Terry, I don't want to go. I don't want anything that has to do with Vietnam."

In the 1960s, American society excoriated Vietnam veterans. When we returned from the war, society ridiculed, trashed, persecuted, spit on, abused, and accused us. As a result, a multitude of Vietnam veterans recoiled from society. Many suffered drug or alcohol addiction and even tragically snuffed out their own life by committing suicide in a desperate effort to end the torment. Many of my fellow veterans remained lost in the 1960s, their life never progressing past that point.

As for me, I spent forty years never thinking of the war, having nothing to do with the military, never identifying with the military, never even going to the VA hospital for help. Nonetheless, Terry kept on urging me.

He said, "I think it will help you to go to the wall and to see."

Terry got on the Internet and found David Berkholz's picture at a virtual Vietnam veterans wall website. He showed it to me. I wept.

Finally, one Monday morning, Terry showed up at our apartment and said, "Pastor Herb, we're going on a surprise trip for a few days, my treat. I already got us hotel rooms."

I thought, "Well, okay. This is a nice little surprise."

After I packed some clothes, we hit the road.

A while later, Terry confessed, "We're headed to the capital, Washington, D.C."

All excitement left me.

Terry continued, "I want you to go with me to see the Vietnam Veterans Memorial."

Adrenaline began to race through my veins, causing my heart to pound in frustration. Taking deep short breaths, I sat there trying to figure out how to get out of this. I had never visited Washington, D.C. and didn't want to offend Terry. Filled with mixed emotion, I looked forward to seeing our nation's capital and appreciated what Terry tried to do for me. He genuinely wanted to help me conquer this issue. However, I didn't want to go to that wall! As we drove nonstop from Nashville to Washington, D.C., we talked about everything but our destination. Late into the evening, we arrived and checked into the hotel. I travailed all night over going to the wall, my efforts to fall asleep futile.

I kept telling myself, "Man! I can't do this! I just can't do this!"

Early the next morning, we drove to the capital mall. Knowing what awaited me there filled me with dread more so than excitement. I sat motionless in the passenger seat of Terry's truck. Captivated by intense angst, I engaged in periodic small talk with Terry to keep all things Vietnam confined to the outer edges of my mind. We arrived at the Vietnam Veterans Memorial about seven o'clock. Terry coaxed me out of the truck. I did not want to go. I had nothing to do with the military or the war or even talked about it for over forty years. I wanted to keep it that way.

Trembling, I slowly walked from the parking area to the wall, a walk that I did not want to make. Yet, things bigger than me compelled me against my will as I took one step after another, just like the walk to the principal's office after hitting Jimmy over the head with the baseball bat, just like when I took my squad out that fateful night of the ambush. As I approached, I only saw an eerie fog lurking about at the memorial, as eerie as the anguish that gripped me.

I thought to myself, "Man, I am so scared!"

No other visitors were at the wall, as if God said, "I am having you here alone with yourself. This is your time to grieve."

I dwelt there by myself for a good while. Finally, I saw a solitary black man standing at one of the directory podiums which listed names and their location on the wall. A veteran of the Vietnam War himself, he wore a hat that said Army. He looked at me with a genuine smile, appreciation gleaming in his eyes.

Welcome home soldier! Thank you for your service.

He came over and said, "I want to tell you something. Welcome home, soldier! Thank you for your service."

He put his arm around me and hugged me. The heaviness of guilt began to dissipate. Condemnation that I had done an evil thing by serving in the Vietnam War began to lose its sting.

He was the first person in my entire life who ever said that to me, "Welcome home, soldier!"

I thought to myself, "Man! For forty years, no one ever said, 'Welcome home.'"

My parents never said, "Welcome home!"

My brothers and sisters never said, "Welcome home!"

There wasn't a soul to be found anywhere in the 1960s who said, "Man, I am glad you are home!"

We talked a bit. He told me that now his mission in life was to greet and comfort Vietnam veterans at the wall every day.

He asked, "Who are you looking for?"

I tried to tell him about David. Despite all my effort, I couldn't form the words. I stood there a complete helpless mute.

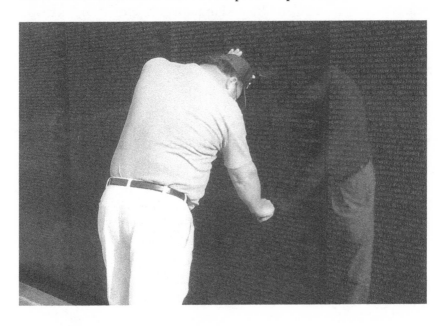

Remembering David Berkholz.

Finally, Terry said, "David Berkholz. We are looking for a Specialist David Berkholz from Michigan."

The man said, "Come on. I'll help you find your buddy."

He looked up David's name in the directory and then took me to panel 14E of the wall. After we found David's name, I just stood there thinking about the night of the ambush. I placed my forearm up against the wall to brace myself, leaned my head against my arm, and wept. After a while, he gave me a piece of paper and a pencil so I could etch David's name from the wall. Deep in my mind, I desperately hoped that maybe David too somehow survived the morgue as I did. But after seeing his name on the wall and etching it onto the paper, I knew for sure that David perished.

My visit to the Vietnam Veterans Memorial ignited a long process of dealing with forty years of suppressed emotional pain, a literal hell that roiled inside me. During my life, I always looked for new things to do, new challenges because I wanted to keep busy, never satisfied with the status quo. Perhaps this drive came from a subconscious desire to avoid thinking about what happened in Vietnam. After forty years of suppression, the Vietnam War loomed fresh in my mind starting the day that I went to the wall. It raged all over again within me.

During the day, I constantly fought off thoughts of the war that emerged from my subconscious. At night, I writhed and convulsed in pure hell, thinking if I did this differently or if I did that differently, then maybe David would have lived. I tossed, turned, and thrashed about all night. It got so bad that I had to sleep in another room. Becky would come in the next morning, and my room looked like a war zone. I spent nights in agony, turmoil, and conflict with little sleep. I stopped going to crowded places by myself. If I sat in a restaurant, I had to have my back to the wall, so I could keep an eye on anyone approaching me. I became more irritable on a regular basis. Becky recognized my suffering and gave me space and covered me with devoted prayer.

I lived this way for four years. I did my best to hide my PTSD and function during the day. But at night when I tried to sleep, I relived the terror all over again. Monday through Friday, I struggled to contain my torment.

On Saturday, I begged God, "Lord, give me a message to preach on Sunday. Just get me through Sunday."

I arranged for other people to preach on Wednesday night. During this time, I didn't preach in the middle of the week much. It took all my strength to make it through the week just to get to

Sunday again. Though I tried to mask the situation, some in the church recognized that I suffered from PTSD.

One day, Becky confronted me about my physical health because I drank unusually large amounts of water and my legs ached tremendously all the time. A man who attended our church brought in a blood sugar testing kit and tested my blood a few times. The results ranged from 400 mg/dl to 600 mg/dl. He told me to go to the hospital before I slipped into a diabetic coma.

I set up an appointment with the local doctor that Becky used. After conducting some tests, the doctor informed me that I had full-blown diabetes. Knowing that I had served at some point in the military, the doctor urged me to go to the VA hospital. After all these years of avoiding everything military, I decided to go.

Much to my surprise, I received excellent care from the VA hospital in Nashville. My primary care doctor, Dr. Karen Jackson, tested me again and confirmed that I had diabetes. She asked me questions about where and when I served in Vietnam to confirm my exposure to Agent Orange. I knew that I got exposed. Back in Vietnam, I saw areas that we operated in get sprayed and two days later all the vegetation died. I had no doubt that I was exposed to Agent Orange, which likely caused my diabetes.

Dr. Jackson kept pressing me to talk with her colleague about my PTSD. She made me appointments, but I never went to speak with the psychologist. Seeking help for PTSD would be an admission of weakness on my part. As a man, I had to show strength, not weakness. As a soldier, I had to show even greater strength and conquer anything that came along. Therefore, I had to control PTSD on my own. Looking back, I believed this to be the reason that most soldiers didn't seek help with their PTSD. In addition to upholding this soldierly creed, I was also a pastor. I'm supposed to help other people with their problems, not have problems myself.

Because of all this, I refused to go to therapy. I ignored Dr. Jackson's advice for about a year. She pleaded with me to go to the next appointment that she set up for me, emphasizing that her colleague worked exclusively with Vietnam veterans.

Dr. Jackson begged, "Just go and talk to her."

Finally, I gave in and attended the next appointment that she set. At that appointment, I met who turned out to be the most wonderful doctor, Elizabeth Fenimore. We had a group session of about fifteen men. Dr. Fenimore asked each one of us a question.

As I sat there, I pouted to myself, "I am not doing this! I am not sitting here with fifteen other guys and talk about my emotional wounds as we refight the Vietnam War. I refuse!"

At the end of the session, as I walked out the door, Dr. Fenimore said, "Mr. Mays, would you stay a few minutes? I want to talk to you."

I obliged her while everyone else departed.

She then continued, "Here's what I want to do for you. I don't normally do this. I normally do group sessions. But I'm going to make an exception for you and do one-on-one sessions with you. Just you and I will go through this therapy."

She never met me before. Why she would do this especially for me, I didn't know.

I thought, "Well, what do I have to lose? At least I won't be in a group." I replied, "Okay, I'll give it a try."

She then said, "We are going to start out really easy to get to know you better, but eventually we are going to talk about your entire experience in Vietnam. You are going to relive every minute of what happened to you over there."

For three hours a week over several months, I went to see Dr. Fenimore. She knew my situation and what happened to me in Vietnam. She read my records.

At our first session, she said, "Mr. Mays, I can help you, but you have to cooperate and work with me."

I replied that I would. At first, we talked about my childhood, my views on life, and how I felt about things. Around the second month, we started talking about my war experience.

With tears streaming down her cheeks, Dr. Fenimore eventually declared, "It's so hard to believe that someone as young as you were could be a sergeant during war time and go through that. I find it amazing that a twenty-year-old boy could do the things that you did." Her sincerity convinced me that she shed genuine tears on my behalf.

Her affirmation made me feel better. I began to see my service in Vietnam as positive and good rather than negative and evil. I started sleeping better at night. Dr. Fenimore earnestly cared about me and applauded my military service to the country. We went through those sessions one by one, which revealed the tremendous pain built up inside me for decades. I had terrible guilt for not bringing David home alive. I promised every soldier in my squad that I would get them home safely. Then I failed David, my best friend, while surviving the war myself. Dr. Fenimore pointed out that even though we lost David, I had brought fourteen other soldiers back alive from that mission in which a larger enemy force pinned us down for over four hours.

Another substantial guilt tormented me because I killed fellow human beings. However, Dr. Fenimore explained that back then, Vietnam War soldiers were young and swore an oath to fight for our country just like the enemy soldiers who tried to kill us did. We all, enemy soldiers included, answered the call of duty to serve our respective country. It was war. We all fought to win and survive amid chaos.

Be that as it may, for many of us, the Vietnam War went far beyond the 1960s and 1970s. Not only did I fight the war in Vietnam, I fought another war internally for forty years. During the therapy sessions, I had to consciously recall the war to let it loose. I grappled with reliving my war experience, often crying tears of grief. Dr. Fenimore cried along with me.

The process took about eight months or so. I would say that I achieved over a 90 percent healing. I still had some issues because PTSD was incurable. I could only hope to minimize and control the symptoms. We all heard the saying "War is hell!" Well, it most definitely was. Combat veterans lived with it all their lives. Every day, I wrestled with thoughts and emotions that made certain situations hard. Fortunately, I no longer fretted during the week hoping that, somehow, I made it to Sunday. Currently, if I had a bad day because of the war, it occurred randomly and seldom. I gave God the glory that He put me in touch with the right person who possessed the right expertise and knowledge to help me. Dr. Fenimore taught me not to focus on the fact that I lived through the war and other didn't, but to focus on my children, grandchildren, and everything else I did in life because I had lived.

I think of all the Vietnam veterans who committed suicide because they had no help. They didn't learn how to cope with the trauma and look for the positive things in their experience and in their life. If they had just humbled themselves and sought God, and if they had just known that God loved them, cared about them, and wanted to help them, then they could have grasped healing. In reality, seeking help had never been a sign of weakness or incompetence as I originally thought. It actually took a lot of courage to reach out. It took a big person to do that. I was (and continue to be) deeply grateful to the VA hospital, Dr. Fenimore, and Dr. Rothschild (her associate) who assisted in the process.

From time to time, I thought about the pain and torment that I suffered by going to the Vietnam Veterans Memorial. I pondered how that event reopened my internal wounds. Sometimes, I felt that it wasn't worth all that turmoil. Had I known the aftermath, I wouldn't have done it. Then, I remembered how my therapy liberated me. Now, I could deal with my war experience and talk about it. Because I finally got help with my PTSD, I was able to author this book. If this book only helped just one person, then going to the wall was worth the pain and suffering.

After I completed the program at the VA hospital, my daughter got me a dog from the pound, which helped me a lot. I named him Furlin. A huskie and a smart dog, Furlin always knew when I had a bad day and cheered me up. Petting his thick fur always made me feel better. He loved to roll over and have his belly rubbed. I talked to him about my problems, and he always listened without talking back. Spending time with Furlin dissolved any stress that I felt. He loved me unconditionally, which made me feel accepted for who I was regardless of flaws. He needed and depended on me, which gave me a sense of value and worth. Furlin lifted my spirits after people dragged me down with petty criticism and complaints.

About two years ago, my grandson and I decided to get a donkey for my grandson to care for. I ended up getting two donkeys, Jack and Pearl. They had the ability to sense my frustration, anger, or heavyheartedness and provide comfort. I soon found myself talking to them on days that I didn't feel well. I started venting my frustrations to them. They politely and eagerly listened to me. When I finished talking, Jack and Pearl brayed in response as if to say we understand and sympathize.

Jack and Pearl encouraged me because donkeys never seem to have bad days. People who had bad days were often unapproachable. But my donkeys never had a bad day. I could always talk to them and feel better afterward. Nowadays, as soon as I go outside, Jack and Pearl started talking. I talked back to them in return. We had conversations. I told people that I talked to my donkeys in English and in tongues. I even prayed with them. They always listened and never talked back. Totally relaxed around my animals, I told them any problem that I had. They never judged, interrupted, or sassed back. They too were a great therapy to me.

Always looking for me, Jack and Pearl came running every time I went outside. They wanted to draw close to me. It reminded me of how God, desiring to draw close, always looked for us. My donkeys always wanted to be near me. God constantly looked for people who wanted to draw close to Him. Evidently, Jack and Pearl even helped me better understand spiritual truths.

I titled this book *He, Me, and My Donkeys* because all of them meant so much to me. My Father-God is the only real father that I ever knew. He gave me a great family, great friends, and a great church. Yet, I still encountered bad days. When dealing with frustrations, I just went to the field and talked to my donkeys. They were one of the most effective therapies that I ever had.

CHAPTER 14

Nuggets of Truth

1. No person has a meaningless life.

Absolutely no insignificant people exist in this world. God has a purpose for each and every person. God does great things through unassuming people. God used this scrawny, stuttering, poor farm boy to positively touch the life of many. Growing up with little expectation of amounting to anything, I have served in the army, fought in a war, coached youth for a decade, had two successful businesses, got a college degree, shared the Gospel in domestic and foreign lands, and pastored for two decades. For every one of these things, I give God entirely all the glory because His hand has been on my life. For my part, I submitted to and allowed God to have His hand on me.

The greatest impact one can have on mankind is to do acts of love and goodness to those they encountered in daily life. The smallest act of kindness is written in God's books in Heaven. Don't think for a minute that what one does for others doesn't pack a powerful punch for humanity. Therefore, live a meaningful life doing good to others by allowing God to be in charge. God creates every person with a divine purpose in life. The only thing that can stand in the way is that person.

In Jeremiah 1:5, God proclaims, "Before I formed you in the womb, I knew you, before you were born I set you apart; I appointed you as a prophet to the nations."

Psalm 139:16 states, "Your eyes saw my unformed body; all the days ordained for me were written in Your book before one of them came to be."

Other sacred scriptures that confirm this are Isaiah 44:24, Jeremiah 29:11, and Psalms 139:13–14. God has a plan for each person's life. All they need do is submit to God's will for that life and see the impact it has on humanity. Seek to live a noble, godly life rather than to grasp at notoriety and fortune. Positively touch the life of those encountered daily even with the smallest of kind gestures.

2. When God opens a door, walk through it.

When God called me into the mission field, I decided at that moment to surrender everything in my life to God no matter what. Submitting to God's will for my life made all the difference. I had no idea how to enter the field of mission work. I had no training, experience, contacts, or supporters when I first started. However, I did have submission to and trust in God. Subsequently, God opened doors for me to walk through. The opportunity to go to Panama on a mission trip opened up. Once there, God caused me to cross paths with people who then offered additional opportunities for me to reach out to the Indians with the Gospel and with love. I never had to lower my shoulder, charge, and bust through a door.

Revelation 3:8 says, "I know your deeds. Behold, I have put before you an open door which no one can shut, because you have a little power, and have kept My word, and have not denied My name."

God may not call a person into ministry. But, however God wants to use a particular life, I beseech that person to submit totally to God. Then faithfully walk through the doors that God opens.

3. Life has ups and downs.

Life simultaneously has ups and downs. Learn to take the good with the bad, the enjoyable with the unpleasant. Praise and worship God to honor Him for the good in life. Use spiritual weapons to deal with the bad.

John 16:33 says, "I have told you these things, so that in Me you may have peace. In this world you will have trouble. But take heart! I have overcome the world."

Sin exists in this world which allows Satan to steal, kill, and destroy. In addition, our own decisions and actions often result in misfortune. Don't blame God. Because mankind sinned, bad things happen in the world. However, God has made a way for us to endure.

Keep your eyes and attention on God. Mathew 14:22–33 tell us that Peter walked on the water toward Jesus during a storm. When Peter took his attention off Jesus and focused on the wind and the waves, he began to sink in the water. By concentrating on his adverse situation, Peter sank. The deep water began to devour him. He was helpless. When Peter called out to the Lord for help, Jesus delivered him.

While attending Bible school, my difficult situation got the best of me because I focused on all my problems. Once I fixed my attention back on God, life became very bearable and I finished college. As an added bonus, the tough times better prepared me for missionary work in the jungle.

Romans 5:3–4 teach, "We rejoice in our sufferings, knowing that suffering produces endurance, and endurance produces character, and character produces hope."

People experience good things in life side by side with bad things. Have peace in Jesus even though faced with trouble. Since Jesus overcame the world, He is well able to see us through anything. Use difficult times as a way to develop yourself. The apostle Paul declared that he learned to be content when he had much in life and when he had little.

4. Be a master at your craft.

Focus on quality when plying your trade. When pastoring the church in Portland, even though we only had about a hundred people attend any given service, Becky and I did our best to give them an excellent experience with God rather than try to attract and entertain a large crowd.

Better to do a few things extremely well than to do a multitude of different things adequately. Pick a few things in life that you love to do and then be a master craftsman at them. Find your passion and then figure out how to make that your life's work. (Hint: If you submit to God, He will open the doors for this.) Then highly develop the skills and abilities involved in doing what you love.

Becky and I have a much greater impact on people's life because we focus on helping those in our sphere of influence, those we encounter daily. This gives our ministry much more meaning than if we superficially touch the life of tens of thousands in a shallow way that quickly evaporates and is forgotten.

God has a purpose for every life. God equips each person with talents and abilities that compliment this divine commission. God also places the passion to do a specific calling in each person. Recognize yours.

5. Seek help with problems.

If you have a problem, get help dealing with it. Problems don't resolve themselves. First turn to God.

As I mentioned earlier, Psalms 121:1–2 say, "I lift up my eyes to the hills—where does my help come from? My help comes from the Lord, the Maker of heaven and earth."

By calling to God and trusting Him, God will bring the right people into your life and open doors for you that you don't even know are there. Once He does, embrace that help and don't hesitate to walk through that door.

We are always stronger working together. No soldier is sent out to attack the enemy solely on one's own. Soldiers go as a team and have support soldiers in the background assisting as well.

Ecclesiastes 4:12 says, "Though one may be overpowered, two can defend themselves. A cord of three strands is not quickly broken."

So why do we soldiers think that we need to solve our personal problems solely on our own? It's just silly pride.

Proverbs 16:18 says, "Pride goes before destruction, a haughty spirit before a fall."

Don't be ashamed to ask for help. I didn't get salvation when I was a deacon because I fretted about what people would think of me. I didn't get help with PTSD for years because I felt that as a pastor, I was the problem solver for people and their issues. Therefore, I should be able to deal with PTSD on my own. I was terribly wrong on both accounts. When I finally got help for PTSD, experts showed me ways to alleviate the torment I experienced and taught me how to manage my memories of the Vietnam War. Humble yourself and seek help starting with God.

BIBLIOGRAPHY

"Average Monthly Social Security Benefits, 1940-2015." InfoPlease. Accessed June 2017. ttps://www.infoplease.com/business-finance /us-economy-and-federal-budget/average-monthly -social-security-benefits-1940-2015.

Wikipedia, the Free Encyclopedia. "Daejeon." Accessed May 2017. https://en.wikipedia.org/wiki/Daejeon.

"Dau Tieng to Ho Chi Minh City." Google Maps. Accessed May 2017. https://www.google.com/maps/dir/Dầu+Tiếng,+Binh+Duong, +Vietnam/Saigon/@11.0819737,106.269016,10z/data=!3m1! 4b1!4m13!4m12!1m5!1m1!1s0x310b4b8d28fb3b17:0xe13b8 6f38f361517!2m2!1d106.4641459!2d11.348909!1m5!1m1!1s 0x317529292e8d3dd1:0xf15f5aad773c112b!2m2!1d106.629 6638!2d10.8230989.

"Distance from Nashville to Panama City (Panama)." Trippy-Travel Questions Answered. Accessed July 2017. https://www.trippy. com/distance/Nashville-to-Panama-City-Panama.

"4th, 25th Divisions Switch Brigades." Ivy Leaf. 35th Infantry Regiment (Cacti) Association. August 13, 1967. http://www. cacti35th.org/regiment/history/other/4th081367.htm.

"FRONTLINE VIETNAM: Armored Cavalry (720p)." *YouTube.* February 3, 2015. https://www.youtube.com/watch?v=1Ssa66R vH3Q.

"General Information-South Korea." Google. Accessed May 2017. http://www.sites.google.com.

Wikipedia, the Free Encyclopedia. "Geography of South Korea." Accessed May 2017. https://en.wikipedia.org/wiki/Geography_of_South _Korea.

Guerrero, Alina. "Escaped Colonel Seized in Panama, 'Coup Attempt' Quashed." AP News Archive. December 5, 1990. http://www. apnewsarchive.com/1990/Escaped-Colonel-Seized-in-Panama-Coup-Attempt-Quashed/id-bafa6abcef301b092b3eecbcd3 094a84.

Hartt, Gary. "One Soldier's Story as Related to a Brother." *Triple Deuce Newsletter*, 2017.

The Holy Bible. n.d.

"The Military Draft During the Vietnam War." Exhibit, Resistance and Revolution: The Anti-Vietnam War Movement at the University of Michigan, 1965-1972. Accessed May 2017. http://michi-ganintheworld.history.lsa.umich.edu/antivietnamwar/exhibits/show/exhibit/draft_protests/the-military-draft-during-the-.

"Minimum Wage Since 1938." CNN Money. Accessed June 2017. http://money.cnn.com/interactive/economy/minimum-wage-since -1938/.

"Oakland Army Base-Gateway to Vietnam." The Original Yesterdays Weapons. Last modified March 4, 2009. https://www.tapatalk.com/groups/steyrmannlicher/oakland-ar-my-base-gateway-to-vietnam-pictures-resi-t6303.html?sid =0e028a0cacd359772f4ab723072919f6.

Schmitt, Eric. "U.S. Helps Quell Revolt in Panama." The New York Times-Breaking News, World News & Multimedia. December 6, 1990. https://www.nytimes.com/1990/12/06/world/us-helps-quell-revolt-in-panama.html.

Wikipedia, the Free Encyclopedia. "USS Admiral H. T. Mayo (AP-125)." Accessed May 2017. https://en.wikipedia.org/wiki/USS_Admiral_H._T._Mayo_(AP-125).

Vida Ministries-Christian Ministry in Panama. Accessed July 2017. http://www.vidaministries.com/.

"Vietnam in HD E02: Search & Destroy (1966-1967) 720P HD." *YouTube.* June 30, 2014. https://www.youtube.com/watch?v=2sI6WzCH_C8.

"William Eldred WARD III's Obituary on The Tennessean." The Tennessean. July 17, 2012. http://www.legacy.com/obituaries/tennessean/obituary.aspx?pid=158599086.

"Yosha Bunko." William Wetherall. Last modified December 18, 2015. http://www.wetherall.org/prose/Wetherall_2015_Kishine_ Barracks.html.

CONTRIBUTION

Writing by Richard Douglas Salcido.

Richard Salcido earned his bachelor of science degree in business management from the California State University, Long Beach, in 1988. After which, he entered active duty in the US Army as a commissioned officer, where he wrote a multitude of military correspondence ranging from orders and memorandums to letters and reports. In the early 1990s, he served as the assistant commandant for the Military Police Training Program at Fort Leonard Wood, Missouri. As law enforcement operations officer, he was responsible for the completeness and accuracy of military police reports. While assigned as an instructor at the Military Police School, located at Fort McClellan, Alabama, he wrote numerous training and lesson plans for the officer basic course. He completed the Instructor Training Couse, the Small Group Leader Instructor Course, and the Army Doctrine Instructor Course.

Upon resigning from the military, Richard revised and taught the fleet operations portion of the driver orientation training program for his employer, a transportation company. He also ghost-wrote letters, memorandums, and e-mails for the president of a small corporation in the construction industry.

Richard has studied the Holy Bible for thirty-six years, teaching at his local church for several of those years. He is currently working on a novel titled *Uriah*, an action-thriller from the perspective of Bathsheba's husband (2 Samuel). It includes romance, espionage, and war.

ABOUT THE AUTHOR

Herbert Mays served in combat during the Vietnam War for the US Army as a twenty-year-old sergeant. Mortally wounded and left for dead in an army morgue, he miraculously woke up a few days later in an army hospital. Following his honorable discharge from the military, he worked for the US Postal Service until retirement. He then started two successful businesses in the construction industry.

In 1993, at the age of forty-seven, Herbert answered the call to full-time ministry. He sold his business, trusted his livelihood to God, and attended Rhema Bible Training College, located in Broken Arrow, Oklahoma. He graduated in 1995 with a ministerial degree in missions. Before year's end, he was in the mountains of Panama, sharing the Gospel of Jesus Christ with the Guaymi Indians, where he saw many miracles occur.

God then called Herbert to start a church in the rural community of Portland, Tennessee. Faithful and submissive to the Holy Spirit, he has pastored there for twenty years, continuing to see the saving grace and miraculous power of God.

CPSIA information can be obtained
at www.ICGtesting.com
Printed in the USA
LVHW110806270220
648337LV00001B/1